TABLE OF CONTENTS

LATER POEMS

SELECTED POEMS OF EDITH SITWELL

By the same author

Poetry

COLLECTED POEMS
GARDENERS AND ASTRONOMERS
THE OUTCASTS

Anthologies

A BOOK OF FLOWERS
PLANET AND GLOW-WORM

Prose

A NOTEBOOK ON WILLIAM SHAKESPEARE
FANFARE FOR ELIZABETH
THE QUEENS AND THE HIVE

(*Macmillan*)

SELECTED POEMS
OF
Edith Sitwell

*Chosen with an introduction
by John Lehmann*

MACMILLAN
London · Melbourne · Toronto
1965

MACMILLAN AND COMPANY LIMITED
St Martin's Street London WC 2
also Bombay Calcutta Madras Melbourne

THE MACMILLAN COMPANY OF CANADA LIMITED
70 Bond Street Toronto 2

PRINTED IN GREAT BRITAIN BY RICHARD CLAY (THE CHAUCER PRESS), LTD.,
BUNGAY, SUFFOLK

ACKNOWLEDGMENTS

THE editor wishes to thank the British Council and the National Book League, in whose series *Writers and Their Work* his introduction originally appeared in a different form.

The poems included in this selection were first published in book form as follows:

'Country Dance', 'Fox Trot', 'Green Geese', 'Kitchen Song' and 'Lullaby for Jumbo' in *Bucolic Comedies*; 'The Strawberry' in *Five Poems*; 'Gold Coast Customs' in *Gold Coast Customs*; 'Jodelling Song' in *Rustic Elegies*; 'The Soldan's Song' and 'Where Reynard-Haired Malinn' in *The Sleeping Beauty*; 'Colonel Fantock', 'Kitchen Song', 'The Drum' and 'The Little Ghost Who Died for Love' in *Troy*, all published by Gerald Duckworth & Co. Ltd.

'Popular Song', published as no. 15 of 'The Ariel Poems' by Faber & Gwyer Ltd.

'Aubade', 'Early Spring' and 'Polka' in *Façade*, published by The Favil Press.

'The Shadow of Cain' in *The Shadow of Cain*, published by John Lehmann Ltd.

'Bagatelle', 'Sailor, What of the Isles?', 'The Blinded Song-Bird near the Battle-Field', 'The Night Wind', 'The Queen of Scotland's Reply', 'The Road to Thebes' and 'You said, "This is the time of the wild spring"' in *Gardeners and Astronomers*; 'Heart and Mind' and 'Invocation' in *Green Song*; 'An Old Woman', 'Lullaby', 'Serenade: Any Man to Any Woman',

'Song: Once My Heart was a Summer Rose', 'Song: We are the Darkness in the Heat of the Day', 'Still Falls the Rain' and 'Street Song' in *Street Songs*; 'A Girl's Song in Winter', 'His Blood Colours my Cheeks', 'La Bella Bona Roba', Praise We Great Men' and 'The Yellow Girl' in *The Outcasts*; 'Eurydice' in *The Song of the Cold*, all published by Macmillan & Co. Ltd.

'A Bird's Song' in *Selected Poems*, 'The Song of the Cold' in *New Writing 23*, and 'Mary Stuart to James Bothwell' in *New Writing 27*, all published by Penguin Books Ltd.

'At the Crossroads' and 'The Death of Prometheus' in *Music and Ceremonies*, published by the Vanguard Press, Inc.

INTRODUCTION

In the course of the history of English literature there have been very few women to make their name as poets. It would, of course, have been exceptional, not to say scandalous in the conditions of the age, to find a female dramatist in Elizabeth's reign; but in the subsequent centuries there was increasingly little to prevent a woman from devoting herself to the muse, and it is curious and surprising that outstanding poets of the female sex are so rare. Everyone will think at once of Emily Brontë and Christina Rossetti, both of whom belong to the nineteenth century; but in the earlier centuries who besides the Duchess of Newcastle and Katharine Phillips are remembered or read today? If such poets even existed, their poems died with them; and yet each of the women whose poetry has survived is an altogether exceptional figure, and her contribution to English poetry both singular and powerful like an azalea of brilliant white or pure red blossoming in a bank of swamp honeysuckle.

Such a figure in our own age was Edith Sitwell. Like Emily Brontë and Christina Rossetti, she came of a remarkable family in which every member has in the same sudden-flowering generation displayed uncommon gifts in one branch or another of literary creation; but unlike those two illustrious predecessors, she came to her unique stature as a poet in the English-speaking world today by a long process of development. Edith Sitwell was writing poetry for nearly sixty years and her work went through many phases; it was always unmistakable for the work of anyone else, and in spite of many sharp differences between one phase and another, always showed a basic unity of inspiration; but, as in the case of another great poet of the twentieth century, W. B. Yeats, the sum of her work is greater than its parts. Her early poetry, like Yeats's, would always have been read for its fresh lyricism, its wit and colour, if she had never written another word after her first two volumes; but her later work is so much more profound and satisfying in its vision of life and displays such control of the technical means, that it reflects some of its glory on what went before; while the interest it has for us is enhanced when we see in it the resolution of contrasting themes from the earlier work and can savour it as the full ripening of a mind and artistic personality of extended and persistent growth.

Edith Sitwell was also an indefatigable and highly original anthologist, and combined the chosen comments of others with her own *obiter dicta* in two unique anthology-journals, *A Poet's Notebook* and *A Notebook on William Shakespeare*. In all these works, or in the introductions to them, she provided a great deal of valuable light on her views of what the lives of poets mean, what poetry is for and how it works; so that they are not only fascinating in themselves but also important for anyone who wishes fully to appreciate the *œuvre* of this remarkable poet. I strongly recommend the readers of this selection to explore them.

There are no short cuts to the appreciation of poetry, though there can be many charts, illustrated itineraries and descriptive milestones. This introduction can, at best, be no more than one of the latter: to appreciate Edith Sitwell's work one must read it, read it through and then read it again. And if one believes, as I do, that to hear a poet recite her own work adds something precious to our understanding of it, then one should listen to as many as possible of the large number of records Dame Edith made during her lifetime. She always had a profound interest in music, and her association with William Walton and other composers who wrote music for such poem sequences as *Façade* resulted not merely in a setting to music but, when she recited herself, in a new artistic creation.

Edith Sitwell's eminence as a poet was generally acknowledged, on both sides of the Atlantic, in the late forties; but it should not be imagined that the path to that eminence was easy. On the contrary, it was a long and obdurate fight with an often uncomprehending and tardy public opinion, though perhaps some of the opposition may have at times been less purposefully embattled than appeared to the always mettlesomely defensive Sitwellian ardour. Nevertheless, even in the days when her flights of metaphor bewildered those of slower imagination, when she maintained in her poetry that light 'creaked' and that rain could 'squawk down' 'grey as a guinea fowl', she found appreciation in plenty from critics and readers of discriminating and forward-looking taste in the arts. She never belonged to any school, except of her own making; she was deeply influenced by the Symbolist movement, but so has been the whole of European poetry, and it would be extraordinary indeed if a poet of such sensitive artistic antennae, with such fertile image-making powers, had not responded to that great release of poetic vigour. Above all, she never remained *set*; and though it may appear a paradox that the daughter of an ancient aristocratic family, the *avant garde* innovating poet of the highly individual 'twenties, should become one of the most eloquent poetic voices of an age of tragic world upheaval and social levelling, such development could always have been envisaged by those who from the first had understood her will-power and restless energy, and her intense, untrammelled awareness.

II

It is often the case that the imaginative roots of an outstanding creative artist have been nourished by an intensely lived childhood, in which exceptional opportunities existed for the early awakening of aesthetic responses — ample libraries a boy or girl can pick and choose in at will, beautiful pictures at home, an active family devotion to music or the theatre, or perhaps the romantic appeal of house and gardens and natural surroundings.

It would probably be a fruitless labour to search for such clues with too meticulous a curiosity; but the description that Sir Osbert Sitwell has given, in his autobiographical work, *The Scarlet Tree*, of the surroundings and exploits of himself, his brother and his sister during their childhood and youth, reveals that the imaginative experiences were indeed there in abundance, and confirms the impression created by Dame Edith's early poetry.

Nevertheless, it is clear from the same work that her childhood was not easy. Her relationship with her parents was not altogether happy; her extreme sensitiveness, her devotion to books and music and lack of interest in the fashionable pursuits of the *grand monde* that surrounded her family in the ancestral home of Renishaw Hall, brought opposition and criticism that might have reduced an ordinary child to sullen, inhibited acquiescence; with the poet, however, it seems only to have increased her determination to live her own life and to withdraw into her inner world.

In her early youth she escaped to Paris with Helen Rootham, who had been appointed her governess, and her stay in the French capital not only had a liberating effect on her spirit but also opened her mind and imagination to French poetry. Miss Rootham was an extremely sensitive student and interpreter of French literature. Her version of Rimbaud's *Les Illuminations* remains one of the finest translations into English of that difficult poet's work, who always remained one of Dame Edith's favourites. She also admitted that one of the strongest influences guiding her towards poetry as a life-task was a first reading of Baudelaire at the age of seventeen, one of those early revelations in artists' lives, the force of which is rarely surpassed in later years. But though France and French literature meant so much, one must not forget another influence, once upon a time the birthright of almost every educated Englishman, which completed the education of a poet who was eventually to receive European acclaim. 'I mention at some length,' says Sir Osbert, 'the effect, and lingering influence, of Italy on my brother, my sister, and myself, because it provides a clue to the work which later we set ourselves — or which set itself for us — and have since striven, however imperfectly, to accomplish. By this path we came to the classical tradition, through the visual arts, rather than through Greek and Latin. In a sense as artists, we thus belong to Italy, hardly less than to England, to that old and famous combination of Italian influence and English blood.'

It would, however, be putting matters into a false perspective to insist too exclusively on Edith Sitwell's direct debt, as an artist, to France or the classical lands of the Mediterranean. She was, above all, deeply rooted in the English tradition, and her *Notebooks* and her anthologies show that the whole of English poetry, from the time of Skelton and Chaucer down to our own century, nourished her poetic spirit. It shows a rare receptivity to differing modes and artistic aims, to know, in one's girlhood, all Pope's *Rape of the Lock* by heart and at the same time to have a passion for Swinburne. The influence of both reveals itself in her work to the attentive ear; and it is no surprise to the reader who has become intimate with the full range of her poetry to find how much space she devotes in the three volumes of her anthology *The Pleasures of Poetry* to the work of Herrick and of Blake, capturing some of the unequalled country freshness of the former and jewel-like imaginative fire of the latter in her own most successful lyrics and songs; to Shelley in his supreme moments of ethereal conjuration; to the purest instance of romantic image-painting in the work of the Pre-Raphaelites, who found their inspiration in Keats; and to the infinitely subtle refinements of Tennyson. The English quality of her poetry is marked, too, by the deep impress of her childhood surroundings: glimpses of the romantic gardens of great English country houses appear in the imagery of innumerable poems, only in the alchemy of her imagination they are gardens that have become the natural setting for legend and fairy tale, where King Midas walks among the auriculas and primulas and Pan is dancing among the strawberry beds, and the gardener is

old as tongues of nightingales
that in the wide leaves tell a thousand Grecian tales.

In such power of transformation, of creating new wonder and significance by the marriage of the familiar with the unexpected symbol already rich in imaginative associations, Edith Sitwell has always excelled. 'The world I see,' she wrote of her early poems, 'is a country world, a universe of growing things, where magic and growth are one.' The deepest inner experiences and discoveries of her childhood were exploited in this process for her poetry; she never lost them; but, equally, she never ceased to add to them. The acquisitive Ariel of her restless mind continually brought new treasures back to its master spirit of poetry, from the works of mystic philosophers, scientists and poets of all lands and all ages. Anyone who wishes to understand how tireless this activity has been should study the notes she added to many of her major poems of the last ten years.

III

In her *Collected Poems* Edith Sitwell wrote of her earliest work: 'At the time I began to write, a change in direction, imagery and rhythms in poetry had become necessary, owing to the rhythmical flaccidity, the verbal deadness, the dead and expected patterns of some of the poetry immediately preceding us.' And she goes on to describe the shock her innovations caused, and the violent opposition they aroused among the conventional readers (and reviewers) of poetry.

It is not too much to say that even today, after four decades during which Edith Sitwell became world famous as a poet, and was formally honoured by three English Universities, these early poems still arouse bewilderment and even opposition in certain quarters, though the frontier of acceptance has been pushed far beyond the small circle of enlightened admirers who understood, when *Bucolic Comedies* and *Façade* were published, that a new poet of rare and exciting gifts had appeared. Many of those who still reject them will acknowledge the power and beauty of the poems of her latest period, from 1940 onwards; and yet the poems which appeared in *Street Songs* and *Green Song* spring as naturally from the early poems as a flower from its bud and, as I have already suggested, cast the most valuable light upon their purpose and meaning.

To escape from 'the dead and expected patterns': there is the key of Edith Sitwell's poetic endeavours in the 'twenties. In *Laughter in the Next Room*, Osbert Sitwell has explained how *Façade* first came to be created: 'The idea of *Façade* first entered our minds as the result of certain technical experiments at which my sister had recently been working: experiments in obtaining through the medium of words the rhythms of dance measures such as waltzes, polkas, foxtrots. These exercises were often experimental enquiries into the effect on rhythm, on speed, and on colour of the use of rhymes, assonances, dissonances, placed outwardly, at different places in the line, in most elaborate patterns.' These experiments — which were indeed exercises but also, more often than not, poems of great fascination in their own right — were extremely various, but they all have

15

relationship with one another through the linking quality of the poet's extremely individual imagination which runs through them all. Both Edith Sitwell and her brother have, in their writings, laid emphasis on the importance of the rhythmical and textual aspect of the experiments; but the novel choice and association of images, which I have already touched upon, is an equally important ingredient in their originality. Reading them through today, one has the impression that a brilliantly gifted child has taken the fragments of Shelley's 'dome of many coloured glass', all the variously strange and lovely things in the world and all the many facets of experience and emotion, and set them together again in fanciful patterns.

Here is an example of the seemingly effortless music, the trans-figured nursery-rhyme world of these early poems:

> Grey as a guinea-fowl is the rain
> Squawking down from the boughs again.
>   'Anne, Anne
>   Go fill the pail,'
> Said the old witch who sat on the rail.
> 'Though there is a hole in the bucket,
> Anne, Anne,
> It will fill my pocket;
> The water-drops when they cross my doors
> Will turn to guineas and gold moidores . . .'

It was just such images as the rain 'grey as a guinea fowl', 'squawking down from the boughs' that woke the clamour of dismay that greeted these poems. 'The fire was furry as a bear', 'the morning light creaks down', 'goats-beard rivers' — Edith Sitwell has latterly given elucidations to these once so 'shocking' conceits, but to a lively imagination they never needed apology. They startle; but it is the business of poetical comparison to startle, and by bringing things together that have never yet met, to refashion thought. And as Shakespeare once thought nothing of bringing a band of English rustics into 'a wood near Athens', so Edith Sitwell following the impulse of her imagination discovered that

> The harsh bray and hollow
> Of the pot and the pan
> Seems Midas defying
> The great god Apollo!

In *Green Geese* there is one of the most beautiful examples of this myth-making — or rather myth-changing power:

> The trees were hissing like green geese . . .
> The words they tried to say were these:
>
> 'When the great Queen Claude was dead
> They buried her deep in the potting shed.'
>
> The moon smelt sweet as nutmeg root
> On the ripe peach-trees' leaves and fruit,
>
> And her sandal-wood body leans upright
> To the gardener's fright, through the summer night.

Edith Sitwell once wrote that: 'In most of the *Bucolic Comedies* there are no technical experiments and usually the rhythm is a drone-sound like that of a hive or the wind in the trees.' Nevertheless, the experiments had begun, were already there in embryo; *Façade* only brought out certain elements of the art of *Bucolic Comedies* and developed them to an extraordinary degree.[1] The conjunction of images becomes as violent as the clash of symbols, as violent as often the effect of the rhythm and the

[1] The original version of *Façade* was privately printed in 1922, a year before the publication of *Bucolic Comedies* (which also contains most of it); but many of the poems in *Bucolic Comedies* were written or in draft before *Façade* was attempted.

clanging bells of the internal rhymes and assonances. There are times when the sequence of word pictures, names and rhymes seems dictated only by the 'free association' of a vivid imagination quickened to the highest pitch of excitement and leaping right over the boundaries of sense; and yet, after several readings, especially when one is mindful of the poems that have gone before and the poems that are to come after, the underlying coherence, the unity of spirit behind them, becomes apparent. Her aim of escaping from the rhythmical flaccidity, the verbal deadness of contemporary tradition, is boldly and brilliantly achieved. What could be less 'Tennysonian' (in the decadent sense of the word) than *Fox Trot*:

> Old
> > Sir
> > > Faulk,
>
> Tall as a stork,
> Before the honeyed fruits of dawn were ripe, would walk,
> And stalk with a gun
> The reynard-coloured sun,
> Among the pheasant-feathered corn the unicorn has torn, forlorn the
> Smock-faced sheep
> Sit
> > And
> > > Sleep:
> Periwigged as William and Mary, weep . . .
> 'Sally, Mary, Mattie, what's the matter, why cry?'
> The huntsman and the reynard-coloured sun and I sigh . . .

This was shock-treatment with a vengeance for the sleepy-sickness of poetry; but always one feels a deeper consequence underneath the surface inconsequence (as in the 'nonsense' poems of Edward Lear), and sometimes a note of strange sadness and mystery comes hauntingly through, as in *Jumbo Asleep*. In reading *Façade* one should remember that the poems were eventually assembled for William Walton's music, and for dramatic presentation: they are wonderfully adapted for their purpose, and gain from it as well. It is a stimulating and thrilling experience to be present when they are performed; and the memory of the absurd scandal of the first night has become part of the period flavour that enhances the delight they give—the period of the triumphs of jazz, of Ronald Firbank's novels, of Diaghilev's final conquest of the artistic world of the West.

One of the most interesting things about Edith Sitwell's art is the way in which all aspects of it seem to be present at every stage of her development, while at each stage one particular aspect becomes dominant. At the next stage, in *The Sleeping Beauty* (1924), she turned away from the satirical inventions of *Façade*, and devoted herself to the exploitation of the elegiac, romantic vein which she had already begun to work in *Bucolic Comedies*.[1] The contrast at first sight between the world of Don Pasquito and Mr. Belaker, 'the allegro, negro cocktail-shaker', and *The Soldan's Song*, with its Elizabethan and Keatsian echoes, could scarcely be sharper:

> When green as a river was the barley,
> Green as a river the rye,
> I waded deep and began to parley
> With a youth whom I heard sigh.

[1] A word of caution against myself should here be inserted. I have in the main followed the order of composition given in *The Canticle of the Rose*; but only the most painstaking research into dates of original publications in magazines or booklets long out of print can establish the order of writing of many of the poems, for Edith Sitwell always assumed the privilege of rewriting her poems and inserting the new versions into later books — often without comment. Even such research, however, cannot be entirely conclusive, because some poems were kept unpublished much longer than others.

'I seek', said he, 'a lovely lady,
A nymph as bright as a queen,
Like a tree that drips with pearls her shady
Locks of hair were seen;
And all the river became her flocks
Though their wool you cannot shear,
Because of the love of her flowing locks. . . .'

This romantic period lasted up to the writing of *Gold Coast Customs* at the end of the decade; there are moments when the wit of *Façade* reappears, as it were in a different key; and scattered through these poems one comes across many of the poet's favourite images and persons of her legend.

What is equally interesting is that there are many passages where the mood and the images foretell the great phase that was to begin in 1940. If I had not been reading Edith Sitwell's poems for some time, and were asked where the following two stanzas from *Romance* came in her work, I should find it difficult not to assume they were from one of the long poems in *Green Songs* or *A Song of the Cold*:

And still their love amid this green world grieves:
'The gold light drips like myrrh upon the leaves
And fills with gold those chambers of the South
That were your eyes, that honeycomb your mouth.

And now the undying Worm makes no great stir,
His tight embrace chills not our luxuries
Though the last light perfumes our bones like myrrh
And Time's beat dies. . . .'

Some of the poems of this period are among the most lovely Edith Sitwell ever wrote. In others one feels that her inexhaustible power of verse-spinning has been too little checked by a sense of intellectual form and pattern; such a poem as *Elegy on Dead Fashion* is like some of Shelley's longer poems before the great 1820 volume, full of wonderful passages and flashes of beauty, but cloying to the mind and imagination because the note is too unvaried and the riches are poured out in too indiscriminate a profusion. There are, however, magical exceptions: the tender, nostalgic poem of transfigured autobiography, *Colonel Fantock*, the crystal purity of the song called *The Strawberry*, and, most famous of all, the rustic elegy *The Little Ghost Who Died for Love*, the haunting sadness of which pierces the heart every time one reads it with a fresh pang that survives its reappearances in anthology after anthology:

> Fear not, O maidens, shivering
> As bunches of the dew-drenched leaves
> In the calm moonlight . . . it is the cold sends quivering
> My voice, a little nightingale that grieves.
>
> Now Time beats not, and dead Love is forgotten . . .
> The spirit too is dead and dank and rotten,
>
> And I forget the moment when I ran
> Between my lover and the sworded man. . . .'

The poem rises to an unforgettable climax when the village girl, who was hanged in 1708 for shielding her lover in the duel, prophesies a doom hanging over the world for its corruption:

> '. . . so I sank me down,
> Poor Deborah in my long cloak of brown.
> Though cockcrow marches, crying of false dawns,
> Shall bury my dark voice, yet still it mourns
> Among the ruins — for it is not I
> But this old world, is sick and soon must die!'

In her next phase Edith Sitwell was to write again of this corruption and doom, but in accents from which nostalgia and sadness had been almost completely banished. In the long poem *Gold Coast Customs*, published in 1929, she used again the strong rhythms, the clashing rhymes and assonances of *Façade*, but for an effect far removed from the wit and gaiety of that sequence: the banging, insistent drum-beat that runs through it, the hard, explosive consonants, the vivid images of horror, create an almost unbearable atmosphere of savagery, loathsomeness and spiritual death. The contrast between *Gold Coast Customs* and such poems as *The Soldan's Song* and *The Little Ghost Who Died for Love* is a revelation of the range of Edith Sitwell's poetic powers.

'In this poem,' Dame Edith herself wrote, 'the bottom of the world has fallen out. . . . We see everything reduced to the primal need — the "rich man Judas, brother Cain", and the epitome of his civilization, Lady Bamburgher, are at one with the slum-ignorance and the blackness and superstition of the African swamp. The beating of their fevered hearts and pulses is no more than the beating of the drums that heralded the Customs, as they were called, in Ashantee a hundred years ago, when, at the death of any rich or important person, slaves and poor persons were killed so that the bones of the dead might be washed with human blood. So the spiritual dead-in-life cry for a sacrifice — that of the starved.'

The poem is characteristic of all Edith Sitwell's longer works, in that it has no precise plot as *Venus and Adonis* or *The Ancient Mariner* has a plot or sequence of events; there is rather the statement of various themes, their repetition and mingling in a manner that is more reminiscent of music: structure is there, but it is the structure of images, ideas and emotions that are gradually developed, contrasted and resolved in a deeply moving prophetic cry — as Shelley's themes in the *Ode to the West Wind* are resolved. The poet employs considerable skill in a counterpointing of Lady Bamburgher's parties and the heartless nightmare of the African

rites, so that each appears as a metaphor of the other; and under-
lying them both one senses a third parallel theme, of personal
betrayal and love disgraced. The tremendous strength of the
imaginative realization appears at once:

> One fantee wave
> Is grave and tall
> As brave Ashantee's
> Thick mud wall.
> Munza rattles his bones in the dust,
> Lurking in murk because he must.
>
> Striped black and white
> Is the squealing light;
> The dust brays white in the market place,
> Dead powder spread on a black skull's face.
>
> Like monkey-skin
> Is the sea — one sin
> Like a weasel is nailed to bleach on the rocks
> Where the eyeless mud screeched fawning, mocks
>
> At a negro that wipes
> His knife . . . dug there,
> A bugbear bellowing
> Bone dared rear —
> A bugbear bone that bellows white
> As the ventriloquist sound of light,
>
> It rears at his head-dress of felted black hair
> The one humanity clinging there —
> His eyeless face whitened like black and white bones
> And his beard of rusty
> Brown grass cones. . . .

This atmosphere of macabre horror and cruelty is sustained through nearly sixty stanzas in which the rhythm is varied with the utmost mastery, so that in spite of the terrible compulsion of the underlying drum-beat the mind is never wearied. Only occasionally does the poet allow the vision of what is lost, of a fulfilment of longing, to break in:

> O far horizons and bright blue wine
> And majesty of the seas that shine,
> Bull-bellowing waves that ever fall
> Round the god-like feet and the goddess tall!
>
> A great yellow flower
> With the silence shy
> To the wind from the islands
> Sighs 'I die' . . .

It is impossible in this remarkable poem not to be reminded at times, in spite of all surface dissimilarities, of the author of *Atalanta in Calydon*; and to remember that Edith Sitwell in fact confessed to an early passion for Swinburne. Equally, however, W. B. Yeats was surely right when he said that, reading *Gold Coast Customs*, he 'felt that something absent from all literature was back again, and in a form rare in the literature of all generations, passion ennobled by intensity, by endurance, by wisdom. We had it in one man once. He lies in St. Patrick's now under the greatest epitaph in all history.' One should also, I think, remember her own observation: 'I was born by the wildest seas that England knows, and my earliest recollection is of the tides, the wild rush of waves, the sweep onwards, heard night and day, so that it seemed the sound of one's own blood.'

In the great climax Edith Sitwell, having earlier in the poem spoken prophetically of 'the thick sick smoke of London burning', speaks prophetically again, as much of her own coming development, the culminating phase of her art, as of changes in the outside world:

> Yet the time will come
> To the heart's dark slum
> When the rich man's gold and the rich man's wheat
> Will grow in the street, that the starved may eat —
> And the sea of the rich will give up its dead —
> And the last blood and fire from my side will be shed.
> For the fires of God go marching on.

She herself observed that *Gold Coast Customs* was 'written with anguish, and I would not willingly re-live that birth'.

IV

In *Laughter in the Next Room*, Sir Osbert Sitwell says of his sister's life during the 'thirties: 'Alas, after 1929 began the long and mortal illness of our old friend Helen Rootham. And in the next decade, until Helen's death in 1938, the concern my sister felt for her, and the necessity she found herself under to earn money, compelled her to turn away from the natural expression of her being, towards prose: for some ten years she was obliged to abandon poetry. Also her close attendance upon the invalid often prevented her from going with us to Italy.'

It is safe to guess that these years were a time of great spiritual trial and suffering in the life of the poet; a time when the world turned its most hideous face and despair was not far off; the novel (her only novel) which she published in 1936, *I Live Under a Black Sun*, is evidence of this. And yet, compared with *Gold Coast Customs*, the novel seems to have strange sunbursts, interstices of light among the dark clouds, that now suggest that she was gradually making her way back to delight and faith — a new faith deeper than any she had known before.

In January of 1942 Edith Sitwell's first proper volume of poetry for more than a decade, *Street Songs*, was published; and this was followed two years later by *Green Song*. The two volumes contained only about three dozen poems, and yet their appearance was, in my opinion, one of the three or four most important literary events of the war years. *Street Songs* opens with three poems which were immediately felt to express the deepest emotions of that time of darkness and endurance, transmuted by an imagination that used symbols with consummate mastery. The bitter irony of *Serenade*, with its transposition of Marlowe's 'Come live with me and be my love' into the terms of Europe at war, where the lover must be unfaithful because he is 'the cannon's mate' and 'death's cold puts the passion out', and the only serenade is 'the wolfish howls the starving made' is matched by the nightmare symbolism of *Lullaby*, where there is nothing left in the world but the monster 'the Babioun', which sings to the abandoned child on a desecrated earth:

> 'Do, do, do do —
> Thy mother's hied to the vaster race:
> The Pterodactyl made its nest
> And laid a steel egg in her breast —
> Under the Judas-coloured sun.
> She'll work no more, nor dance, nor moan,
> And I am come to take her place
> Do, do.'

These two terrible poems are contrasted with *Still Falls the Rain*, one of the most memorable of all Edith Sitwell's poems, written of the air-raids on Britain in 1940 and moving with a deep pulse of funeral solemnity:

Still falls the Rain —
Dark as the world of man, black as our loss —
Blind as the nineteen hundred and forty nails
Upon the Cross.

In this poem the poet openly declares her Christian faith and conceives the falling of the bombs as a rain which is at the same time the falling of blood from Christ's side; a rain which thus becomes a symbol of punishment and suffering and redemption through that suffering. In the last line Christ speaks: 'Still do I love, still shed my innocent light, my Blood, for thee.'

In the extreme tensity of emotion held within their art, in their technical virtuosity and the force of their imagery, these three poems proclaimed that Edith Sitwell had returned to poetry with her powers undiminished, indeed enhanced. What was perhaps more significant, she seemed able to approach her tremendous theme — at a time when complaints were loud that no war poetry worthy of the cataclysm was being written — through symbols that needed no special intimacy with the esoteric fancy characteristic even of *Gold Coast Customs*, but could be apprehended directly and universally. How valuable a gain this was, can be seen most clearly from *An Old Woman*, the last poem in *Street Songs* and at the same time the first complete realization of the new mode of Sibylline utterance to which the other poems show her feeling her way.

The unprecedented series of long odes in the grand manner, of which *An Old Woman* is the first example, is continued in *Green Song* and *A Song of the Cold* with increasing artistic assurance and skill. Underlying their structure is an iambic line of five beats, the traditional form of English recitative poetry; but this is occasionally increased to six or even seven or eight beats, and at rare intervals reduced to four or three; rhyme — or rather end-rhyming, for her lines are full of subtle hints of

internal rhyming and assonance — is discarded, but her medium
is far removed from the free verse of our time, which has come
to mean little more than prose statement on which an additional
system of sense-pauses is imposed by division into lines. There is
rhythmic life and shape in every one of these poems, of the most
supple and breathing sort, and they seem to evolve organically,
and differently in every instance, out of the heart of the poem's
conception. The long, flowing lines with their apparent ease and
simplicity, their movement as of a swan floating on a softly
gliding river that can suddenly turn to a majestic drumming of
wings across the sky as the bird rises into flight, are the culmina-
tion of Edith Sitwell's lifetime of devoted apprenticeship to her
art. She had always been intensely aware of the importance
of music and texture in the making of verse, as her studies of
other poets' technique had repeatedly shown; in these odes she
handled sound and texture to create poetic effects of the most
astonishing variety and complexity; to find any comparable
achievement one must look beyond her beloved Walt Whitman
to the later work of William Blake, such as *The Book of Thel*.

In this final phase of her art Edith Sitwell used symbols of
the widest range, from Christian and Classical history and
legend, from the Old Testament, and even beyond — from the
primitive pre-history and shadowy beliefs and customs on
which our civilization was gradually built; and she married these
with the more ancient and universal symbols of animal and
flower and corn, gold and precious metal, sea and sun and
stars. It is by such means that she managed to convey in these
odes such an extraordinary sense of depth in Time and Space,
of wisdom ripening in eternal contemplation from a mountain-
top vantage point. The 'golden woman grown old', symbol for
the poet-philosopher who through long personal suffering and
identification with the sufferings of others has reached a vision
beyond the accidents of history, is inspired to see that all created

things are sacred; that if death and darkness are necessary to the order of the universe, there is also eternal renewal, of the spiritual as well as of the physical world; and that behind the evil and terror of the world there is divine forgiveness and charity. The heart of the poet's vision, of her thought, would seem to be the quite simple idea — simple, yet so often lost sight of, and seldom so beautifully expressed, an idea that unites her with the great Christian mystics and the English mystical poets of the seventeenth century — that as the world of nature is transformed and re-created again and again by the action of the sun, so Love transforms and conquers all our sufferings, all the passing triumphs of its opposite, so that 'all in the end is harvest'. Of all the poems of this period, *Eurydice* has perhaps the most exultant declaration of this faith:

Fire on the hearth! Fire in the Heavens! Fire in the hearts of
  men!
I who was welded into bright gold in the earth by Death
Salute you! All the weight of Death in all the world
Yet does not equal Love — the great compassion
For the fallen dust and all fallen creatures, quickening
As is the Sun in the void firmament.
It shines like fire, O bright gold of the heat of the Sun
Of Love across dark fields — burning away rough husks of
  Death
Till all is fire, and bringing all to harvest!

It would be easy to assume that such a philosophy of reconciliation and peace-in-love might lead the poet to an under-estimate of the real and terrible tragedies and horrors of the world. With Edith Sitwell the very opposite was the case. The poems that follow *An Old Woman*, *Harvest*, *Invocation* and *Eurydice* present the problem of evil with unequalled imaginative power. In reading *A Song of the Cold* and the three poems on the age of the atom bomb, in particular *The Shadow of Cain*, one has the feeling that the poet has a presentiment of a terrifying crisis and cataclysm in the history of man. In her symbolism the heart, the heat of the blood has always represented good, and cold — 'the ultimate cold within the heart of man' — evil; and Dives and Lazarus, the craving for riches and the destitute sore-covered human condition (never, it is interesting to observe, the lust for power and the humble misery of powerlessness) are always opposed to one another; and now Dives seems to be about to triumph and his gold to banish the other gold, the gold of the ear of corn that is life.

The Shadow of Cain has been well called, by Sir Kenneth Clark, this 'craggy, mysterious, philosophic poem', and its conclusion, in the dialogue between Dives and Lazarus, 'the poet's deepest and most passionate statement of her concern with original sin'. And what is most remarkable about it is that, as she approaches the awe-inspiring manifestations of evil and destruction, as in *Still Falls the Rain* her instinct is not to despair, but to call upon the most powerful symbols of love she knows, the symbols of Christianity: 'He walks again on the Seas of Blood, He comes in the terrible Rain' is the last line of the poem.

The years since the conclusion of the Second World War have been a time of vast political and economic transformation affecting the circumstances of almost every human being alive. Yet the volcanic shift in the balance of power among nations and empires has not affected them more than the change in the spiritual climate in which they live. This has been so swift, so revolutionary that it appears, not unnaturally, to have had a numbing effect on the higher faculties of man. The war, in the end, found its voice in the work of many poets and novelists; but the peace, the victory, the defeat, the bewilderment in defeat and the heart-breaking disappointment in victory, the apocalyptic manifestation of atomic power — the poets would seem, for a long time, to have been too dazed to speak of them. In those early years only Edith Sitwell dared to face this challenge in her art. The three great poems of the atom bomb lift man to the level of the drama of our time.

I have remarked before on the fact that, though each phase of Edith Sitwell's poetry seems distinctly marked off from those that preceded it, the more carefully one studies them, the more closely one sees that they are related. They are like a continuing argument between the two poles of her inspiration, between romance and satire, affirmation and irony; now one gains the ascendancy, now the other, in method as in content. In her poems from *Still Falls the Rain* to *The Canticle of the Rose* they seem to find a resolution within a larger synthesis: the depth of tenderness and compassion, the understanding of human desolation that so poignantly informed *The Little Ghost Who Died for Love* are there, and at the same time the savage mockery of *Gold Coast Customs*; the dream-like incantations of *The Sleeping Beauty* and the hard drum-beat of rhythms first evolved in *Nursery Rhymes*.

The last two volumes of poetry which Edith Sitwell published were *Gardeners and Astronomers* (1953) and *The Outcasts* (1962), in the American edition called *Music and Ceremonies* (1963) with the addition of several poems not included in *The Outcasts*. After the culmination and resolution of the poems collected in *The Song of the Cold* (1945) and *The Shadow of Cain* (1947), one might have been forgiven for thinking that anything more in this exalted manner must be an anticlimax. At this point one must face one of the difficulties inherent in Dame Edith's poetry. The weight of the English tradition since the Romantic revival has led the public to expect from its poets, especially in their shorter works, poems which transmute into imaginative substance particular experiences and emotions 'recollected in tranquillity'. Such are the lyrics and sonnets, for instance, of Wordsworth,

Matthew Arnold, Thomas Hardy and Edward Thomas. There are almost no such poems in Edith Sitwell's *œuvre*. The emotion is indeed there, but it is as it were at a further remove, and generalized or put into the mouth of some historical or fanciful character.

For this reason, the poems in any one phase are apt to resemble one another rather closely, because even when, as in the case of *Still Falls the Rain* or *The Shadow of Cain*, a specific event inspires them, the mood and the symbols remain much the same. This way of approaching poetry has brought the accusation that she overworks her symbolism, and is constantly repeating herself. My own view is that this criticism is, on the whole, mistaken; that one should consider her later poems more as one long poem in a number of sections, or movements. This does not mean that they altogether escape the danger of excess, and some sympathetic critics have felt that she added little to her achievement after the high-water mark of *The Shadow of Cain* and *Eurydice*. Even so, no one, I believe, can read the last two volumes without feeling that they represent a step beyond the previous work; in such poems as *The Death of Prometheus* and *At the Crossroads* one finds a hitherto unheard, savage bitterness of contempt for what is petty in life in its struggle against what is generous and noble; and in several of the songs, such as *La Bella Bona Roba* and *The Yellow Girl*, a lyrical impulse making new discoveries of astonishing freshness and resonance.

JOHN LEHMANN

EARLY POEMS I

(from *Bucolic Comedies, Sleeping Beauty* and *Façade*)

Early Spring

THE wooden chalets of the cloud
Hang down their dull blunt ropes to shroud

Red crystal bells upon each bough
(Fruit-buds that whimper). No winds slough

Our faces, furred with cold like red
Furred buds of satyr springs, long dead!

The cold wind creaking in my blood
Seems part of it, as grain of wood;

Among the coarse goat-locks of snow
Mamzelle still drags me, to and fro;

Her feet make marks like centaur hoofs
In hairy snow; her cold reproofs

Die, and her strange eyes look oblique
As the slant crystal buds that creak.

If she could think me distant, she
In the snow's goat-locks certainly

Would try to milk those teats, the buds,
Of their warm sticky milk — the cuds

Of strange long-past fruit-hairy springs —
The beginnings of first earthy things.

Aubade

JANE, Jane,
Tall as a crane,
The morning light creaks down again;

Comb your cockscomb-ragged hair,
Jane, Jane, come down the stair.

Each dull blunt wooden stalactite
Of rain creaks, hardened by the light,

Sounding like an overtone
From some lonely world unknown.

But the creaking empty light
Will never harden into sight,

Will never penetrate your brain
With overtones like the blunt rain.

The light would show (if it could harden)
Eternities of kitchen garden,

Cockscomb flowers that none will pluck,
And wooden flowers that 'gin to cluck.

In the kitchen you must light
Flames as staring, red and white,

As carrots or as turnips, shining
Where the cold dawn light lies whining.

Cockscomb hair on the cold wind
Hangs limp, turns the milk's weak mind. . . .
    Jane, Jane,
    Tall as a crane,
    The morning light creaks down again!

Two Kitchen Songs

I

THE harsh bray and hollow
Of the pot and the pan
Seems Midas defying
The great god Apollo!
The leaves' great golden crowns
Hang on the trees;
The maids in their long gowns
Hunt me through these.
Grand'am, Grand'am,
From the pan I am

Flying . . . country gentlemen
Took flying Psyche for a hen
And aimed at her; then turned a gun
On harmless chicken-me — for fun.
The beggars' dogs howl all together,
Their tails turn to a ragged feather;
Pools, like mirrors hung in garrets,
Show each face as red as a parrot's,
Whistling hair that raises ire
In cocks and hens in the kitchen fire!
Every flame shrieks cockle-doo-doo
(With their cockscombs flaring high too);
The witch's rag-rug takes its flight
Beneath the willows' watery light:
The wells of water seem a-plume —
The old witch sweeps them with her broom —
All are chasing chicken-me. . . .
But Psyche — where, oh where, is she?

II

GREY as a guinea-fowl is the rain
Squawking down from the boughs again.
 'Anne, Anne,
  Go fill the pail,'
Said the old witch who sat on the rail.
'Though there is a hole in the bucket,
Anne, Anne,
It will fill my pocket;
The water-drops when they cross my doors
Will turn to guineas and gold moidores. . . .'
The well-water hops across the floors;
Whimpering, 'Anne' it cries, implores,

36

And the guinea-fowl-plumaged rain,
Squawking down from the boughs again,
Cried, 'Anne, Anne, go fill the bucket,
There is a hole in the witch's pocket —
And the water-drops like gold moidores,
Obedient girl, will surely be yours.
So, Anne, Anne,
Go fill the pail
Of the old witch who sits on the rail!'

Green Geese

THE trees were hissing like green geese . . .
The words they tried to say were these:

'When the great Queen Claude was dead
They buried her deep in the potting-shed.'

The moon smelt sweet as nutmeg-root
On the ripe peach-trees' leaves and fruit,

And her sandal-wood body leans upright,
To the gardener's fright, through the summer night.
.   .   .   .   .

The bee-wing'd warm afternoon light roves
Gilding her hair (wooden nutmegs and cloves),

And the gardener plants his seedsman's samples
Where no wild unicorn herd tramples —

In clouds like potting-sheds he pots
The budding planets in leaves cool as grots,

For the great Queen Claude when the light's gilded gaud
Sings Miserere, Gloria, Laud.

But when he passes the potting-shed,
Fawning upon him comes the dead —

Each cupboard's wooden skeleton
Is a towel-horse when the clock strikes one,

And light is high — yet with ghosts it winces
All night 'mid wrinkled tarnished quinces,

When the dark air seems soft down
Of the wandering owl brown.

They know the clock-faced sun and moon
Must wrinkle like the quinces soon

(That once in dark blue grass dew-dabbled
Lay) . . . those ghosts like turkeys gabbled

To the scullion baking the Castle bread —
'The Spirit, too, must be fed, be fed;

Without our flesh we cannot see —
Oh, give us back Stupidity!' . . .

But death had twisted their thin speech,
It could not fit the mind's small niche —

Upon the warm blue grass outside,
They realized that they had died.

Only the light from their wooden curls roves
Like the sweet smell of nutmegs and cloves

Buried deep in the potting-shed,
Sighed those green geese, 'Now the Queen is dead.'

Where Reynard-Haired Malinn

WHERE reynard-haired Malinn
Walks by rock and cave,
The Sun, a Chinese mandarin,
Came dripping from the wave.

'Your hair seems like the sunrise
O'er Persia and Cathay —
A rose-red music strange and dim
As th' embalmèd smile of seraphim.'

He said to her by the white wave
In the water-pallid day
(A forest of white coral boughs
Seemed the delicate sea-spray):

'In envy of your brighter hair, —
Since, Madam, we must quarrel —
I've changed the cold flower-lovely spray
To branches of white coral;

And when, white muslin Madam, you
Coquette with the bright wind,
I shall be but thin rose-dust;
He will be cold, unkind.'

The flowers that bud like rain and dream
On thin boughs water-clear,
Fade away like a lovely music
Nobody will hear,

And Aeolus and Boreas
Brood among those boughs,
Like hermits haunting the dark caves
None but the wise man knows.

But Malinn's reynard-coloured hair,
Amid the world grown sere
Still seemed the Javanese sunrise
Whose wandering music will surprise
Into cold bird-chattering cries
The Emperor of China
Lying on his bier.

The Drum

(*The Narrative of the Demon of Tedworth*)

In his tall senatorial,
Black and manorial,
House where decoy-duck

Dust doth clack —
Clatter and quack
To a shadow black, —
Said the musty Justice Mompesson,
'What is that dark stark beating drum
That we hear rolling like the sea?'
'It is a beggar with a pass
Signed by you.' 'I signed not one.'
They took the ragged drum that we
Once heard rolling like the sea;
In the house of the Justice it must lie
And usher in Eternity.

   .   .   .   .   .

Is it black night?
Black as Hecate howls a star
Wolfishly, and whined
The wind from very far.

In the pomp of the Mompesson house is one
Candle that lolls like the midnight sun,
Or the coral comb of a cock; . . . it rocks. . . .
Only the goatish snow's locks
Watch the candles lit by fright
One by one through the black night.

Through the kitchen there runs a hare —
Whinnying, whines like grass, the air;
It passes; now is standing there
A lovely lady . . . see her eyes —
Black angels in a heavenly place,
Her shady locks and her dangerous grace.

'I thought I saw the wicked old witch in
The richest gallipot in the kitchen!'
A lolloping galloping candle confesses.
'Outside in the passage are wildernesses
Of darkness rustling like witches' dresses.'

Out go the candles one by one
Hearing the rolling of a drum!

What is the march we hear groan
As the hoofèd sound of a drum marched on
With a pang like darkness, with a clang
Blacker than an orang-outang?
'Heliogabalus is alone, —
Only his bones to play upon!'

The mocking money in the pockets
Then turned black . . . now caws
The fire . . . outside, one scratched the door
As with iron claws, —

Scratching under the children's bed
And up the trembling stairs . . . 'Long dead'
Moaned the water black as crape.
Over the snow the wintry moon
Limp as henbane, or herb paris,
Spotted the bare trees; and soon
Whinnying, neighed the maned blue wind
Turning the burning milk to snow,
Whining it shied down the corridor —
Over the floor I heard it go
Where the drum rolls up the stair, nor tarries.

Lullaby for Jumbo

JUMBO asleep!
Grey leaves thick-furred
As his ears, keep
Conversations blurred.
Thicker than hide
Is the trumpeting water;
Don Pasquito's bride
And his youngest daughter
Watch the leaves
Elephantine grey:
What is it grieves
In the torrid day?
Is it the animal
World that snores
Harsh and inimical
In sleepy pores? —
And why should the spined flowers
Red as a soldier
Make Don Pasquito
Seem still mouldier?

Country Dance

THAT hobnailed goblin, the bob-tailed Hob,
Said, 'It is time I began to rob.'
For strawberries bob, hob-nob with the pearls
Of cream (like the curls of the dairy girls),
And flushed with the heat and fruitish-ripe
Are the gowns of the maids who dance to the pipe.
Chase a maid?
She's afraid!
'Go gather a bob-cherry kiss from a tree,
But don't, I prithee, come bothering me!'
She said —
As she fled.
The snouted satyrs drink clouted cream
'Neath the chestnut-trees as thick as a dream;
So I went,
And I leant,
Where none but the doltish coltish wind
Nuzzled my hand for what it could find.
As it neighed,
I said,
'Don't touch me, sir, don't touch me, I say!
You'll tumble my strawberries into the hay.'
Those snow-mounds of silver that bee, the spring,
Has sucked his sweetness from, I will bring
With fair-haired plants and with apples chill
For the great god Pan's high altar . . . I'll spill
Not one!
So, in fun,
We rolled on the grass and began to run
Chasing that gaudy satyr the Sun;

44

Over the haycocks, away we ran
Crying, 'Here be berries as sunburnt as Pan!'
But Silenus
Has seen us. . . .
He runs like the rough satyr Sun.

> Come away!

Fox Trot

Old
   Sir
      Faulk,
Tall as a stork,
Before the honeyed fruits of dawn were ripe, would walk
And stalk with a gun
The reynard-coloured sun,
Among the pheasant-feathered corn the unicorn has torn, forlorn the
Smock-faced sheep
Sit
  And
     Sleep;
Periwigged as William and Mary, weep . . .
'Sally, Mary, Mattie, what's the matter, why cry?'
The huntsman and the reynard-coloured sun and I sigh;
'Oh, the nursery-maid Meg
With a leg like a peg
Chased the feathered dreams like hens, and when they laid an egg
In the sheepskin
Meadows

Where
The serene King James would steer
Horse and hounds, then he
From the shade of a tree
Picked it up as spoil to boil for nursery tea,' said the mourners.
    In the
Corn, towers strain,
Feathered tall as a crane,
And whistling down the feathered rain, old Noah goes again —
An old dull mome
With a head like a pome,
Seeing the world as a bare egg,
Laid by the feathered air; Meg
Would beg three of these
For the nursery teas
Of Japhet, Shem, and Ham; she gave it
Underneath the trees,
Where the boiling
Water
  Hissed,
Like the goose-king's feathered daughter — kissed
Pot and pan and copper kettle
Put upon their proper mettle,
Lest the Flood — the Flood — the Flood begin again through
    these!

Polka

'"Tra la la la —
         See me dance the polka,"
Said Mr. Wagg like a bear,
"With my top-hat

And my whiskers that —
(Tra la la la) trap the Fair.

Where the waves seem chiming haycocks
I dance the polka; there
Stand Venus' children in their gay frocks, —
Maroon and marine, — and stare

To see me fire my pistol
Through the distance blue as my coat;
Like Wellington, Byron, the Marquis of Bristol,
Buzbied great trees float.

While the wheezing hurdy-gurdy
Of the marine wind blows me
To the tune of 'Annie Rooney', sturdy,
Over the sheafs of the sea;

And bright as a seedsman's packet
With zinnias, candytufts chill,
Is Mrs. Marigold's jacket
As she gapes at the inn door still,

Where at dawn in the box of the sailor,
Blue as the decks of the sea,
Nelson awoke, crowed like the cocks,
Then back to the dust sank he.

And Robinson Crusoe
Rues so
The bright and foxy beer, —
But he finds fresh isles in a Negress' smiles, —
The poxy doxy dear,

As they watch me dance the polka,"
Said Mr. Wagg like a bear,
"In my top-hat and my whiskers that, —
Tra la la, trap the Fair.

Tra la la la la —
Tra la la la la —
Tra la la la la la la la la
                La
                La
                La!"'

Jodelling Song

'WE bear velvet cream,
Green and babyish
Small leaves seem; each stream
Horses' tails that swish,

And the chimes remind
Us of sweet birds singing,
Like the jangling bells
On rose-trees ringing.

Man must say farewell
To parents now,
And to William Tell,
And Mrs. Cow.

Man must say farewells
To storks and Bettes,
And to roses' bells,
And statuettes.

Forests white and black
In spring are blue
With forget-me-nots,
And to lovers true

Still the sweet bird begs
And tries to cozen
Them: "Buy angels' eggs
Sold by the dozen."

Gone are clouds like inns
On the gardens' brinks,
And the mountain djinns, —
Ganymede sells drinks;

While the days seem grey,
And his heart of ice,
Grey as chamois, or
The edelweiss,

And the mountain streams
Like cowbells sound —
Tirra lirra, drowned
In the waiter's dreams

Who has gone beyond
The forest waves,
While his true and fond
Ones seek their graves.'

Popular Song

FOR CONSTANT LAMBERT

LILY O'GRADY,
Silly and shady,
Longing to be
A lady,
Walked by the cupolas, gables in the
Lake's Georgian stables,
In a fairy tale like the heat intense,
And the mist in the woods when across the fence
The children gathering strawberries
Are changed by the heat into Negresses,
Though their fair hair
Shines there
Like gold-haired planets, Calliope, Io,
Pomona, Antiope, Echo and Clio.
Then Lily O'Grady,
Silly and shady,
Sauntered along like a
Lazy lady:
Beside the waves' haycocks her gown with tucks
Was of satin the colour of shining green ducks,
And her fol-de-rol
Parasol
Was a great gold sun o'er the haycocks shining,
But she was a Negress black as the shade
That time on the brightest lady laid.
Then a satyr, dog-haired as trunks of trees,
Began to flatter, began to tease,
And she ran like the nymphs with golden foot
That trampled the strawberry, buttercup root,

In the thick gold dew as bright as the mesh
Of dead Panope's golden flesh,
Made from the music whence were born
Memphis and Thebes in the first hot morn,
— And ran, to wake
In the lake,
Where the water-ripples seem hay to rake.
And Adeline,
Charlottine,
Round rose-bubbling Victorine,
And the other fish
Express a wish
For mastic mantles and gowns with a swish;
And bright and slight as the posies
Of buttercups and of roses,
And buds of the wild wood-lilies
They chase her, as frisky as fillies.
The red retriever-haired satyr
Can whine and tease her and flatter,
But Lily O'Grady,
Silly and shady,
In the deep shade is a lazy lady;
Now Pompey's dead, Homer's read,
Heliogabalus lost his head,
And shade is on the brightest wing,
And dust forbids the bird to sing.

EARLY POEMS II
(Before 1940)

The Little Ghost Who Died for Love

FOR ALLANAH HARPER

Deborah Churchill, born in 1678, was hanged in 1708 for shielding her lover in a duel. His opponent was killed, her lover fled to Holland, and she was hanged in his stead, according to the law of the time. The chronicle said, 'Though she died at peace with God, this malefactor could never understand the justice of her sentence, to the last moment of her life.'

'FEAR not, O maidens, shivering
As bunches of the dew-drenched leaves
In the calm moonlight . . . it is the cold sends quivering
My voice, a little nightingale that grieves.

Now Time beats not, and dead Love is forgotten . . .
The spirit too is dead and dank and rotten,

And I forget the moment when I ran
Between my lover and the sworded man —

Blinded with terror lest I lose his heart.
The sworded man dropped, and I saw depart

Love and my lover and my life . . . he fled
And I was strung and hung upon the tree.
It is so cold now that my heart is dead
And drops through time . . . night is too dark to see

Him still. . . . But it is spring; upon the fruit-boughs of your lips,
Young maids, the dew like India's splendour drips;
Pass by among the strawberry beds, and pluck the berries
Cooled by the silver moon; pluck boughs of cherries

That seem the lovely lucent coral bough
(From streams of starry milk those branches grow)
That Cassiopeia feeds with her faint light,
Like Aethiopia ever jewelled bright.

Those lovely cherries do enclose
Deep in their sweet hearts the silver snows,

And the small budding flowers upon the trees
Are filled with sweetness like the bags of bees.

Forget my fate . . . but I, a moonlight ghost,
Creep down the strawberry paths and seek the lost

World, the apothecary at the Fair.
I, Deborah, in my long cloak of brown
Like the small nightingale that dances down
The cherried boughs, creep to the doctor's bare
Booth . . . cold as ivy is the air,

And, where I stand, the brown and ragged light
Holds something still beyond, hid from my sight.

Once, plumaged like the sea, his swanskin head
Had wintry white quills . . . "Hearken to the Dead . . .
I was a nightingale, but now I croak
Like some dark harpy hidden in night's cloak,
Upon the walls; among the Dead, am quick;
Oh, give me medicine, for the world is sick;
Not medicines, planet-spotted like fritillaries,
For country sins and old stupidities,

Nor potions you may give a country maid
When she is lovesick . . . love in earth is laid,
Grown dead and rotten" . . . so I sank me down,
Poor Deborah in my long cloak of brown.
Though cockcrow marches, crying of false dawns,
Shall bury my dark voice, yet still it mourns
Among the ruins, — for it is not I
But this old world, is sick and soon must die!'

The Strawberry

BENEATH my dog-furred leaves you see
The creeping strawberry
In a gold net
The footprints of the dew have made more wet.

Mahomet resting on a cloud of gold
Dreamed of the strawberry
Made of the purpling gauzy heat
And jasper dust trod by his golden feet. —

The jasper dust beside
The fountain tide,
The water jacynth-cold,
The water-ripples like mosaics gold
Have made my green leaves wide and water-cold.

From palaces among the widest leaves
My Sun, my Fatima,
Shows her gold face and sighs,
And darkness dies.

At noon my Fatima, my bright gazelle,
Walks by each gauzy bell
Of strawberries made of such purpling air
As the heat knows, and there

When Fatima, my dew with golden foot,
Comes like all the music of the air
Then shine my berries till those golden footsteps die —
Like all the glittering desert of the air when the hot sun goes by.

The Soldan's Song

WHEN green as a river was the barley,
Green as a river the rye,
I waded deep and began to parley
With a youth whom I heard sigh.
'I seek', said he, 'a lovely lady,
A nymph as bright as a queen,
Like a tree that drips with pearls her shady
Locks of hair were seen;
All the rivers became her flocks
Though their wool you cannot shear,
Because of the love of her flowing locks.
The kingly sun like a swain
Came strong, unheeding of her scorn,
Wading in deeps where she has lain,
Sleeping upon her river lawn
And chasing her starry satyr train.

She fled, and changed into a tree, —
That lovely fair-haired lady . . .
And now I seek through the sere summer
Where no trees are shady.'

Colonel Fantock

TO OSBERT AND SACHEVERELL SITWELL

THUS spoke the lady underneath the trees:
I was a member of a family
Whose legend was of hunting — (all the rare
And unattainable brightness of the air) —
A race whose fabled skill in falconry
Was used on the small song-birds and a winged
And blinded Destiny. . . . I think that only
Winged ones know the highest eyrie is so lonely.
There in a land, austere and elegant,
The castle seemed an arabesque in music;
We moved in an hallucination born
Of silence, which like music gave us lotus
To eat, perfuming lips and our long eyelids
As we trailed over the sad summer grass,
Or sat beneath a smooth and mournful tree.

And Time passed, suavely, imperceptibly.

But Dagobert and Peregrine and I
Were children then; we walked like shy gazelles
Among the music of the thin flower-bells.
And life still held some promise, — never ask
Of what, — but life seemed less a stranger, then,

Than ever after in this cold existence.
I always was a little outside life —
And so the things we touch could comfort me;
I loved the shy dreams we could hear and see —
For I was like one dead, like a small ghost,
A little cold air wandering and lost.
All day within the straw-roofed arabesque
Of the towered castle and the sleepy gardens wandered
We; those delicate paladins the waves
Told us fantastic legends that we pondered.

And the soft leaves were breasted like a dove,
Crooning old mournful tales of untrue love.

When night came, sounding like the growth of trees,
My great-grandmother bent to say good-night,
And the enchanted moonlight seemed transformed
Into the silvery tinkling of an old
And gentle music-box that played a tune
Of Circean enchantments and far seas;
Her voice was lulling like the splash of these.
When she had given me her good-night kiss,
There, in her lengthened shadow, I saw this
Old military ghost with mayfly whiskers, —
Poor harmless creature, blown by the cold wind,
Boasting of unseen unreal victories
To a harsh unbelieving world unkind:
For all the battles that this warrior fought
Were with cold poverty and helpless age —
His spoils were shelters from the winter's rage.
And so for ever through his braggart voice,
Through all that martial trumpet's sound, his soul
Wept with a little sound so pitiful,

Knowing that he is outside life for ever
With no one that will warm or comfort him. . . .
He is not even dead, but Death's buffoon
On a bare stage, a shrunken pantaloon.
His military banner never fell,
Nor his account of victories, the stories
Of old apocryphal misfortunes, glories
Which comforted his heart in later life
When he was the Napoleon of the schoolroom
And all the victories he gained were over
Little boys who would not learn to spell.
All day within the sweet and ancient gardens
He had my childish self for audience —
Whose body flat and strange, whose pale straight hair
Made me appear as though I had been drowned —
(We all have the remote air of a legend) —
And Dagobert my brother whose large strength,
Great body and grave beauty still reflect
The Angevin dead kings from whom we spring;
And sweet as the young tender winds that stir
In thickets when the earliest flower-bells sing
Upon the boughs, was his just character;
And Peregrine the youngest with a naïve
Shy grace like a faun's, whose slant eyes seemed
The warm green light beneath eternal boughs.
His hair was like the fronds of feathers, life
In him was changing ever, springing fresh
As the dark songs of birds . . . the furry warmth
And purring sound of fires was in his voice
Which never failed to warm and comfort me.

And there were haunted summers in Troy Park
When all the stillness budded into leaves;

We listened, like Ophelia drowned in blond
And fluid hair, beneath stag-antlered trees;
Then, in the ancient park the country-pleasant
Shadows fell as brown as any pheasant,
And Colonel Fantock seemed like one of these.
Sometimes for comfort in the castle kitchen
He drowsed, where with a sweet and velvet lip
The snapdragons within the fire
Of their red summer never tire.
And Colonel Fantock liked our company;
For us he wandered over each old lie,
Changing the flowering hawthorn, full of bees,
Into the silver helm of Hercules,
For us defended Troy from the top stair
Outside the nursery, when the calm full moon
Was like the sound within the growth of trees.
But then came one cruel day in deepest June,
When pink flowers seemed a sweet Mozartian tune,
And Colonel Fantock pondered o'er a book.
A gay voice like a honeysuckle nook —
So sweet, — said, 'It is Colonel Fantock's age
Which makes him babble.' . . . Blown by winter's rage
The poor old man then knew his creeping fate,
The darkening shadow that would take his sight
And hearing; and he thought of his saved pence
Which scarce would rent a grave. . . . That youthful voice
Was a dark bell which ever clanged 'Too late' —
A creeping shadow that would steal from him
Even the little boys who would not spell —
His only prisoners. . . . On that June day
Cold Death had taken his first citadel.

GOLD COAST CUSTOMS

Gold Coast Customs

TO HELEN ROOTHAM

In Ashantee, a hundred years ago, the death of any rich or important person was followed by several days of national ceremonies, during which the utmost licence prevailed, and slaves and poor persons were killed that the bones of the deceased might be washed with human blood. These ceremonies were called Customs.

ONE fantee wave
Is grave and tall
As brave Ashantee's
Thick mud wall.
Munza rattles his bones in the dust,
Lurking in murk because he must.

Striped black and white
Is the squealing light;
The dust brays white in the market-place,
Dead powder spread on a black skull's face.

Like monkey-skin
Is the sea — one sin
Like a weasel is nailed to bleach on the rocks
Where the eyeless mud screeched fawning, mocks

At a Negro that wipes
His knife . . . dug there,
A bugbear bellowing
Bone dared rear —
A bugbear bone that bellows white
As the ventriloquist sound of light,

It rears at his head-dress of felted black hair
The one humanity clinging there —
His eyeless face whitened like black and white bones
And his beard of rusty
Brown grass cones.

Hard blue and white
Cowrie shells (the light
Grown hard) outline
The leopard-skin musty
Leaves that shine
With an animal smell both thick and fusty.

One house like a rat-skin
Mask flaps fleet
In the sailor's tall
Ventriloquist street
Where the rag houses flap —
Hiding a gap.

Here, tier on tier
Like a black box rear
In the flapping slum
Beside Death's docks.
I did not know this meaner Death
Meant this: that the bunches of nerves still dance
And caper among these slums, and prance.

'Mariners, put your bones to bed!'
But at Lady Bamburgher's parties each head,
Grinning, knew it had left its bones
In the mud with the white skulls . . . only the grin
Is left, strings of nerves, and the drum-taut skin.

When the sun in the empty
Sky is high
In his dirty brown and white
Bird-skin dress —
He hangs like a skull
With a yellow dull
Face made of clay
(Where tainted, painted, the plague-spots bray)
To hide where the real face rotted away.

So our worm-skin and paper masks still keep,
Above the rotting bones they hide,
The marks of the Plague whereof we died:
The belief,
The grief,
The love,
Or the grin
Of the shapeless worm-soft unshaping Sin —
Unshaping till no more the beat of the blood
Can raise up the body from endless mud
Though the hell-fires cold
As the worm, and old,
Are painted upon each unshaped form —
No more man, woman, or beast to see —
But the universal devouring Worm.

When the sun of dawn looks down on the shrunken
Heads, drums of skin, and the dead men drunken,

I only know one half of my heart
Lies in that terrible coffin of stone,
My body that stalks through the slum alone.
And that half of my heart
That is in your breast
You gave for meat
In the sailor's street
To the rat that had only my bones to eat.

But those hardened hearts
That roll and sprawl,
In a cowl of foul blind monkey-skin,
Lest the whips of the light crash roaring in —
Those hearts that roll
Down the phantom street
They have for their beat
The cannibal drums
And the cries of the slums,
And the Bamburgher parties — they have them all!

One high house flaps . . . taps
Light's skin drum —
Monkey-like shrunk
On all fours now come
The parties' sick ghosts, each hunting himself —
Black gaps beneath an ape's thick pelt,

Chasing a rat,
Their soul's ghost fat
Through the Negro swamp,
Slum hovel's cramp,
Of Lady Bamburgher's parties above
With the latest grin, and the latest love,

And the latest game:
To show the shame
Of the rat-fat soul to the grinning day
With even the rat-skin flayed away.

Now, a thick cloud floating
Low o'er the lake,
Millions of flies
Begin to awake,
With the animation
Of smart conversation:
From Bedlam's madness the thick gadflies
Seek for the broken statue's eyes.

Where the mud and the murk
Whispering lurk:
'From me arises everything,
The Negro's louse,
The armadillo,
Munza's bone and his peccadillo' —

Where flaps degraded
The black and sated
Slack macerated
And antiquated
Beckoning Negress
Nun of the shade,
And the rickety houses
Rock and rot,
Lady Bamburgher airs
That foul plague-spot
Her romantic heart

From the cannibal mart,
That smart Plague-cart
Lady Bamburgher rolls where the foul news-sheet
And the shambles for souls are set in the street.

And stuck in front
Of this world-tall Worm,
Stuck in front
Of this world's confession —
Like something rolled
Before a procession,
Is the face, a flimsy worm-skin thing
That someone has raked
From the low plague-pit
As a figure-head
For Corruption dead,
And a mask for the universal Worm.

Her ape-skin yellow
Tails of hair
Clung about her bone-white bare
Eyeless mask that cackled there:

The Worm's mask hid
Her eyeless mud,
Her shapeless love,
The plot to escape
From the God-ordained shape

And her soul, the cannibal
Amazon's mart,
Where in squealing light
And clotted black night
On the monkey-skin black and white striped dust they
Cackle and bray to the murdered day.

And the Amazon queen
With a bone-black face
Wears a mask with an ape-skin beard; she grinds
Her male child's bones in a mortar, binds
Him for food, and the people buy. For this

Hidden behind
The Worm's mask grown
White as a bone
Where eyeholes rot wide
And are painted for sight,
And the little mouth red as a dead Plague-spot
On that white mask painted to hide Death's rot,

For this painted Plague-cart's
Heart, for this
Slime of the Worm that paints her kiss
And the dead men's bones round her throat and wrist,
The half of my heart that lay in your breast
Has fallen away
To rot and bray
With the painted mud through the eyeless day.

The dust of all the dead can blow
Backwards and forwards, to and fro
To cover the half of my heart with death's rot,
Yet the dust of that other half comes not
To this coffin of stone that stalks through the slum;
Though love to you now is the deaf Worm's lust
That, cloven in halves, will re-unite
Foulness to deadness in the dust
And chaos of the enormous night.

How far is our innocent paradise,
The blue-striped sand,
Bull-bellowing band
Of waves, and the great gold suns made wise
By the dead bays and the horizons grand.

Can a planet tease
With its great gold train,
Walking beside the pompous main —
That great gold planet the heat of the Sun
Where we saw black Shadow, a black man, run,
So a Negress dare
Wear long gold hair?
The Negress Dorothy one sees
Beside the caverns and the trees,
Where her parasol
Throws a shadow tall
As a waterfall —
The Negress Dorothy still feels
The great gold planet tease her brain.

And dreaming deep within her blood
Lay Africa like the dark in the wood;
For Africa is the unhistorical,
Unremembering, unrhetorical,
Undeveloped spirit involved
In the conditions of nature — Man,
That black image of stone hath delved
On the threshold where history began.

Now under the cannibal
Sun is spread
The black rhinoceros-hide of the mud
For endlessness and timelessness . . . dead

Grass creaks like a carrion-bird's voice, rattles,
Squeaks like a wooden shuttle. Battles
Have worn this deserted skeleton black
As empty chain armour . . . lazily back
With only the half of its heart it lies
With the giggling mud devouring its eyes,
Naught left to fight
But the black clotted night
In its heart, and ventriloquist squealing light.

But lying beneath the giggling mud
I thought there was something living, the bray
Of the eyeless mud can not betray —
Though it is buried beneath black bones
Of the fetiches screeching like overtones
Of the light, as they feel the slaves' spilt blood.

In tiers like a box
Beside the docks
The Negro prays,
The Negro knocks.
'Is Anyone there?'
His mumblings tear
Nothing but paper walls, and the blare
Of the gaping capering empty air.
The cannibal drums still roll in the mud
To the bones of the king's mother laved in blood
And the trophies with long black hair, shrunken heads
That drunken, shrunk upon tumbled beds.

The Negro rolls
His red eyeballs,
Prostrates himself.
The Negro sprawls:

His God is but a flat black stone
Upright upon a squeaking bone.

The Negro's dull
Red eyeballs roll . . .
The immortality of the soul
Is but black ghosts that squeak through the hole
That once seemed eyes in Munza's skull.
This is his god:
The cannibal sun
On bones that played
For evermore,
And the dusty roar
Of the ancient Dead,
And the squealing rat,
The soul's ghost fat.

But Lady Bamburgher's Shrunken Head,
Slum hovel, is full of the rat-eaten bones
Of a fashionable god that lived not
Ever, but still has bones to rot:
A bloodless and an unborn thing
That cannot wake, yet cannot sleep,
That makes no sound, that cannot weep,
That hears all, bears all, cannot move —
It is buried so deep
Like a shameful thing
In that plague-spot heart, Death's last dust-heap.

.   .   .   .   .

A tall house flaps
In the canvas street,
Down in the wineshop
The Amazons meet

With the tall abbess
Of the shade. . . .
A ghost in a gown
Like a stiff brigade

Watches the sailor
With a guitar
Lure the wind
From the islands far.

O far horizons and bright blue wine
And majesty of the seas that shine,
Bull-bellowing waves that ever fall
Round the god-like feet and the goddess tall!

A great yellow flower
With the silence shy
To the wind from the islands
Sighs 'I die'.

At the foot of the steps
Like the navy-blue ghost
Of a coiling Negro,
In dock slums lost,

(The ghost haunting steamers
And cocktail bars,
Card-sharpers, schemers,
And Pullman cars)

A ripple rose
With mud at its root
And weeping kissed
A statue's foot.

In the sailor's tall
Ventriloquist street
The calico dummies
Flap and meet:
Calculate: 'Sally go
Pick up a sailor.'
Behind that façade
The worm is a jailer.

'I cannot stiffen . . . I left my bones
Down in the street: no overtones
Of the murdered light can join my dust
To my black bones pressed in the House of Lust.
Only my feet still walk in the street;
But where is my heart and its empty beat?
"Starved silly Sally, why dilly and dally?"
The dummies said when I was a girl.
The rat deserts a room that is bare,
But Want, a cruel rat gnawing there
Ate to the heart, all else was gone,
Nothing remained but Want alone.
So now I'm a gay girl, a calico dummy,
With nothing left alive but my feet
That walk up and down in the Sailor's Street.

Behind the bawdy hovels like hoardings
Where harridans peer from the grovelling boarding
House, the lunatic
Wind still shakes
My empty rag-body, nothing wakes;
The wind like a lunatic in a fouled
Nightgown, whipped those rags and howled.
Once I saw it come
Through the canvas slum,

Rattle and beat what seemed a drum,
Rattle and beat it with a bone.
O Christ, that bone was dead, alone.
Christ, who will speak to such ragged Dead
As me, I am dead, alone and bare,
They expose me still to the grinning air,
I shall never gather my bones and my dust
Together (so changed and scattered, lost . . .)
So I can be decently burièd!
What is that whimpering like a child
That this mad ghost beats like a drum in the air?
The heart of Sal
That once was a girl
And now is a calico thing to loll
Over the easy steps of the slum
Waiting for something dead to come.'

From Rotten Alley and Booble Street,
The beggars crawl to starve near the meat
Of the reeling appalling cannibal mart,
And Lady Bamburgher, smart Plague-cart.
Red rag face and a cough that tears
They creep through the mud of the docks from their lairs;
And when the dog-whining dawn light
Nosed for their hearts, whined in fright,
With a sly high animal
Whimpering, half-frightened call
To worlds outside our consciousness,
It finds no heart within their dress.
The Rat has eaten
That and beaten
Hope and love and memory,
At last, and even the will to die.

But what is the loss? For you cannot sell
The heart to those that have none for Hell
To fatten on . . . or that cheap machine,
And its beat would make springs for the dancing feet
Of Lady Bamburgher down in the street
Of her dogs that nose out each other's sin,
And grin, and whine, and roll therein.

Against the Sea-wall are painted signs
'Here for a shilling a sailor dines'.
Each Rag-and-Bone
Is propped up tall
(Lest in death it fall)
Against the Sea-wall.
Their empty mouths are sewed up whole
Lest from hunger they gape and cough up their soul.
The arms of one are stretched out wide. . . .
How long, since our Christ was crucified?

Rich man Judas,
Brother Cain,
The rich men are your worms that gain
The air through seething from your brain;
Judas, mouldering in your old
Coffin body, still undying
As the Worm, where you are lying
With no flesh for warmth, but gold
For flesh, for warmth, for sheet:
Now you are fleshless, too, as these
That starve and freeze,
Is your gold hard as Hell's huge polar street,
Is the universal blackness of Hell's day so cold?

   .   .   .   .   .

When, creeping over
The Sailor's Street
Where the houses like rat-skin
Masks flap, meet
Never across the murdered bone
Of the sailor, the whining overtone
Of dawn sounds, slaves
Rise from their graves,
Where in the corpse-sheet night they lay
Forgetting the mutilating day,
Like the unborn child in its innocent sleep.
Ah Christ, the murdered light must weep —
(Christ that takest away the sin
Of the world, and the rich man's bone-dead grin)
The light must weep
Seeing that sleep
And those slaves rise up in their death-chains, part
The light from the eyes
The hands from the heart,
Since their hearts are flesh for the tall
And sprawling
Reeling appalling
Cannibal mart,
But their hands and head
Are machines to breed
Gold for the old and the greedy Dead.

I have seen the murdered God look through the eyes
Of the drunkard's smirched
Mask as he lurched
O'er the half of my heart that lies in the street
'Neath the dancing fleas and the foul news-sheet.

Where (a black gap flapping,
A white skin drum)
The cannibal houses
Watch this come —
Lady Bamburgher's party; for the plan
Is a prize for those that all fours ran
Through the rotting slum
Till those who come
Could never guess from the mud-covered shapes
Which are the rich or the mired dire apes,
As they run where the souls, dirty paper are blown
In the hour before dawn, through this long hell of stone.

Perhaps if I too lie down in the mud,
Beneath tumbrils rolling
And mad skulls galloping
Far from their bunches of nerves that dance
And caper among these slums and prance,
Beneath the noise of that hell that rolls,
I shall forget the shrunken souls,
The eyeless mud squealing 'God is dead',
Starved men (bags of wind) and the harlot's tread,
The heaven turned into monkey-hide
By Lady Bamburgher's dancing fleas,
Her rotting parties and death-slack ease,
And the dead men drunken
(The only tide)
Blown up and down
And tossed through the town
Over the half of my heart that lies
Deep down, in this meaner Death, with cries.
The leaves of black hippopotamus-hide

Black as the mud
Cover the blood
And the rotting world. Do we smell and see

The sick thick smoke from London burning,
Gomorrah turning
Like worms in the grave,
The Bedlam daylight's murderous roar,
Those pillars of fire the drunkard and whore,
Dirty souls boiled in cannibal cookshops to paper
To make into newspapers, flags? . . . They caper
Like gaping apes. Foul fires we see,
For Bedlam awakes to reality.

The drunkard burning,
The skin drums galloping,
In their long march still parched for the sky,
The Rotten Alleys where beggars groan
And the beggar and his dog share a bone;
The rich man Cain that hides within
His lumbering palaces where Sin
Through the eyeless holes of Day peers in,
The murdered heart that all night turns
From small machine to shapeless Worm
With hate, and like Gomorrah burns —
These put the eyes of Heaven out,
These raise all Hell's throats to a shout,
These break my heart's walls toppling in,
And like a universal sea
The nations of the Dead crowd in.

Bahunda, Banbangala, Barumbe, Bonge,
And London fall, . . . rolling human skin drums

Surrounded by long black hair, I hear
Their stones that fall,
Their voices that call,
Among the black and the bellowing bones.

But yet when the cannibal
Sun is high
The sightless mud
Weeps tears, a sigh,
To rhinoceros-hided leaves: 'Ah why
So sightless, earless, voiceless, I?'

The mud has at least its skulls to roll;
But here as I walk, no voices call,
Only the stones and the bones that fall;
But yet if only one soul would whine,
Rat-like from the lowest mud, I should know
That somewhere in God's vast love it would shine:
But even the rat-whine has guttered low.

I saw the Blind like a winding-sheet
Tossed up and down through the blind man's street
Where the dead plague-spot
Of the spirit's rot
On the swollen thick houses
Cries to the quick,
Cries to the dark soul that lies there and dies
In hunger and murk, and answers not.

Gomorrah's fires have washed my blood —
But the fires of God shall wash the mud
Till the skin drums rolling
The slum cries sprawling

And crawling
Are calling
'Burn thou me!'
Though Death has taken
And pig-like shaken,
Rooted, and tossed
The rags of me.
Yet the time will come
To the heart's dark slum
When the rich man's gold and the rich man's wheat
Will grow in the street, that the starved may eat, —
And the sea of the rich will give up its dead —
And the last blood and fire from my side will be shed.
For the fires of God go marching on.

LATER POEMS
(*from 1940 onwards*)

Invocation

FOR ALEC AND MERULA GUINNESS

I WHO was once a golden woman like those who walk
In the dark heavens — but am now grown old
And sit by the fire, and see the fire grow cold,
Watch the dark fields for a rebirth of faith and of wonder.

The turning of Ixion's wheel the day
Ceased not, yet sounds no more the beat of the heart
But only the sound of ultimate Darkness falling
And of the Blind Samson at the Fair, shaking the pillars of the
    world and emptily calling.

For the gardeners cried for rain, but the high priests howled
For a darker rain to cool the delirium of gold
And wash the sore of the world, the heart of Dives,
Raise wheat for the hunger that lies in the soul of the poor —
Then came the thunderous darkness

And the fly-like whispering of small hopes, small fears,
The gossips of mean Death — gadflies and gnats, the summer
    world:

The small and gilded scholars of the Fly
That feed upon the crowds and their dead breath
And buzz and stink where the bright heroes die
Of the dust's rumours and the old world's fevers.
Then fell the world in winter.

But I, a golden woman like the corn goddess
Watch the dark fields, and know when spring begins
To the sound of the heart and the planetary rhythm,
Fires in the heavens and in the hearts of men,
Young people and young flowers come out in the darkness.
And where are they going? How should I know? I see only
The hierarchies love the young people — the Swan has given his
    snows
And Berenice her wild mane to make their fair hair,
And speaking of love are the voices that come from the darkness:

Of the nobler love of Man for his brother Man,
And of how the creeds of the world shall no more divide them
But every life be that of a country Fate
Whose wheel had a golden woof and warp, the Day —
Woven of threads of the common task; and light
Tells to that little child the humble dust
Tales of the old world's holiness, finds veins of ore
In the unripe wheat-ear; and the common fire
That drops with seed like the Sun's, is fallen from the long-leaved
    planets.

So when the winter of the world and Man's fresh Fall
When democratic Death feared no more the heart's coldness
Shall be forgotten,
O Love, return to the dying world, as the light
Of morning, shining in all regions, latitudes
And households of high heaven within the heart.

Be then our visible world, our world invisible!
Throughout our day like the laughing flames of the Sun
Lie on our leaves of life, your heat infusing
Deep in the amber blood of the smooth tree.

The panic splendour of the animal
Is yours — O primal Law
That rules the blood — (the solar ray in the veins,
The fire of the hearth, the household Deity
That shines not, nor does it burn, destroy like fire,
But nourishes with its endless wandering
Like that of the Golden Ones in the high heavens.)

Rule then the spirit working in dark earth
As the Sun and Planets rule the husbandman —
O pride that in each semitone
Of amber blood and bone
Proclaims the splendour that arose from the first Dark!

Be too the ear of wheat to the Lost Men
Who ask the city stones if they are bread
And the stones of the city weep. . . .

                                        You, the lost days
When all might still be hoped for, and the light
Laid gold in the unhopeful path of the poor —
The shrunken darkness in the miser's heart.

Now falls the night of the world: — O Spirit moving upon the
    waters
Your peace instil
In the animal heat and splendour of the blood —

(The hot gold of the sun that flames in the night
And knows not down-going
But moves with the revolutions in the heavens.)

The thunders and the fires and acclamations
Of the leaves of spring are stilled, but in the night
The Holy Ghost speaks in the whispering leaves.
O wheat-ear shining like a fire and the bright gold,
O water brought from far to the dying gardens!

Bring peace to the famine of the hearts and lips,
And to the Last Man's loneliness
Of those who dream they can bring back sight to the blind!
You are the Night
When the long hunt for Nothing is at rest
In the Blind Man's Street, and in the human breast
The hammer of Chaos is stilled.
                                        Be then the sleep
When Judas gives again the childish kiss
That once his mother knew — and wash the stain
From the darkened hands of the universal Cain

An Old Woman

I, AN old woman in the light of the sun,
Wait for my Wanderer, and my upturned face
Has all the glory of the remembering Day,
The hallowed grandeur of the primeval clay
That knew the Flood, and suffered all the dryness
Of the uncaring heaven, the sun its lover.

For the sun is the first lover of the world,
Blessing all humble creatures, all life-giving,
Blessing the end of life and the work done,
The clean and the unclean, ores in earth, and splendours
Within the heart of man, that second sun.

For when the first founts and deep waterways
Of the young light flow down and lie like peace
Upon the upturned faces of the blind
From life, it comes to bless
Eternity in its poor mortal dress —
Shining upon young lovers and old lechers
Rising from their beds, and laying gold
Alike in the unhopeful path of beggars
And in the darkness of the miser's heart.
The crookèd has a shadow light made straight,
The shallow places gain their strength again —
And desert hearts, waste heavens, the barren height
Forget that they are cold.
The man-made chasms between man and man
Of creeds and tongues are fill'd, the guiltless light
Remakes all men and things in holiness.

And he who blessed the fox with a golden fleece,
And covered earth with ears of corn like the planets
Bearded with thick ripe gold,
For the holy bread of mankind, blessed my clay:
For the sun cares not that I am a simple woman,
To him, laughing, the veins in my arms and the wrinkles
From work on my nursing hands are sacred as branches
And furrows of harvest . . . to him, the heat of the earth
And beat of the heart are one, —
Born from the energy of the world, the love

That keeps the Golden Ones in their place above,
And hearts and blood of beasts ever in motion, —
Without which comets, sun, plants, and all living beings
And warmth in the inward parts of the earth would freeze.
And the sun does not care if I live in holiness,
To him, my mortal dress
Is sacred, part of the earth, a lump of the world
With my splendours, ores, impurities, and harvest,
Over which shines my heart, that ripening sun.

Though the dust, the shining racer, overtake me,
I too was a golden woman like those that walk
In the fields of the heavens: — but am now grown old
And must sit by the fire and watch the fire grow cold,
— A country Fate whose spool is the household task.
Yet still I am loved by the sun, and still am part
Of earth. In the evenings bringing home the workers,
Bringing the wanderer home and the dead child,
The child unborn and never to be conceived,
Home to the mother's breast, I sit by the fire
Where the seed of gold drops dead and the kettle simmers
With a sweet sound like that of a hive of bees;
And I wait for my Wanderer to come home to rest —
Covered with earth as if he had been working
Among the happy gardens, the holy fields
Where the bread of mankind ripens in the stillness.
Unchanged to me by death, I shall hold to my breast
My little child in his sleep, I shall seem the consoling
Earth, the mother of corn, nurse of the unreturning.

Wise is the earth, consoling grief and glory,
The golden heroes proud as pomp of waves, —
Great is the earth embracing them, their graves,
And great is the earth's story.

For though the soundless wrinkles fall like snow
On many a golden cheek, and creeds grow old
And change, — man's heart, that sun,
Outlives all terrors shaking the old night:
The world's huge fevers burn and shine, turn cold,
Yet the heavenly bodies and young lovers burn and shine,
The golden lovers walk in the holy fields
Where the Abraham-bearded sun, the father of all things,
Is shouting of ripeness, and the whole world of dews and splen-
    dours are singing
To the cradles of earth, of men, beasts, harvests, swinging
In the peace of God's heart. And I, the primeval clay
That has known earth's grief and harvest's happiness,
Seeing mankind's dark seed-time, come to bless,
Forgive and bless all men like the holy light.

Eurydice

TO JOHN LEHMANN

Fires on the hearth! Fires in the heavens! Fires in the hearts of
    Men!
I who was welded into bright gold in the earth by Death
Salute you! All the weight of Death in all the world
Yet does not equal Love — the great compassion
For the fallen dust and all fallen creatures, quickening
As is the Sun in the void firmament.
It shines like fire. O bright gold of the heat of the Sun
Of Love across dark fields — burning away rough husks of
    Death
Till all is fire, and bringing all to harvest!

See then! I stand in the centre of my earth
That was my Death, under the zenith of my Sun
Bringing a word from Darkness
That Death too has compassion for all fallen Nature.
For as the Sun buries his hot days and rays
To ripen in earth, so the great rays of the heart
Are ripened to wisdom by Death, and great is our forgiveness.

When through the darkness Orpheus came with his Sun-like
    singing
Like the movements in the heavens that in our blindness
Could we but emulate, would set right our lives —
I came to the mouth of the Tomb, I did not know our meeting
    would be this:
— Only like the return at evening
Of the weary worker in the holy fields, —
The cry of welcome, the remembered kiss!

In the lateness of the season, I with the golden feet
That had walked in the fields of Death, now walk again
The dark fields where the sowers scatter grain
Like tears, or the constellations that weep for the lateness of the
    season —
Where the women walk like mourners, like the Afternoon
    ripened, with their bent heads;
Their golden eyelids like the drifts of the narcissus
In spring, are wet with their tears. They mourn for a young wife
    who had walked these fields
— So young, not yet had Proserpina tied up her golden hair
In a knot like the branchèd corn. . . . So good was she, —
With a voice like the sweet swallow. She lies in the silent
    Tomb

86

And they walk in the fields alone. Then one of the Dead who
    lay
Beneath the earth, like the water-dark, the water-thin
Effigy of Osiris, with a face green as a moon,
— He who was lying in darkness with the wheat
Like a flame springing from his heart, or a gold sound,
Said to me, 'We have been blind and stripped God naked of
    things
To see the light which shines in the dark, and we have learned
That the gold flame of the wheat may spring from a barren
    heart.'

When I came down from the Metropolis of the Corn
Then said the ferine dust that reared about me,
'I have the famine of the lion, all things devour,
Or make them mine. . . . Venus was powerful as me—
Now is she but a handful of dry amber dust;
And my tooth cracked the husk, the dry amber wall
That held the fire of the wheat. That fire is gone, —
And remember this, that Love, or I, have ground
Your heart between the stones of the years, like wheat.'

But as I left the mouth of the Tomb, far off, like the noise of the
    dark wild bees
I heard the sounds arise from the dwellings of Men, and I
    thought of their building,
Their wars, their honey-making, and of the gold roofs built
    against Darkness.

And I had learned beneath the earth that all gold nature
Changes to wheat or gold in the sweet darkness,
Why do they weep for those in the silent Tomb,
Dropping their tears like grain? Her heart, that honeycomb,

Thick Darkness like a bear devours. . . . See, all the gold is gone!
The cell of the honeycomb is six-sided. . . . But there, in the five
    cells of the senses,
Is stored all their gold. . . . Where is it now? Only the wind of
    the Tomb can know.
But I feared not that stilled and chilling breath
Among the dust. . . . Love is not changed by Death,
And nothing is lost and all in the end is harvest.

As the earth is heavy with the lion-strong Sun
When he has fallen, with his hot days and rays,
We are heavy with Death, as a woman is heavy with child,
As the corn-husk holds its ripeness, the gold comb
Its weight of summer. . . . But as if a lump of gold had changed
    to corn,
So did my Life rise from my Death. I cast the grandeur of Death
    away
And homeward came to the small things of Love, the building
    of the hearth, the kneading of daily bread,
The cries of birth, and all the weight of light
Shaping our bodies and our souls. Came home to youth,
And the noise of summer growing in the veins,
And to old age, a serene afternoon,
An element beyond time, or a new climate.

I with the other young who were born from darkness,
Returning to darkness, stood at the mouth of the Tomb
With one who had come glittering like the wind
To meet me — Orpheus with the golden mouth,
You — like Adonis born from the young myrrh-tree, you, the
    vine-branch
Broken by the wind of love. . . . I turned to greet you —
And when I touched your mouth, it was the Sun.

Still Falls the Rain

The Raids, 1940. Night and Dawn

STILL falls the Rain —
Dark as the world of man, black as our loss —
Blind as the nineteen hundred and forty nails
Upon the Cross.

Still falls the Rain
With a sound like the pulse of the heart that is changed to the
    hammer-beat
In the Potter's Field, and the sound of the impious feet

On the Tomb:
                    Still falls the Rain
In the Field of Blood where the small hopes breed and the
    human brain
Nurtures its greed, that worm with the brow of Cain.

Still falls the Rain
At the feet of the Starved Man hung upon the Cross.
Christ that each day, each night, nails there, have mercy on us —
On Dives and on Lazarus:
Under the Rain the sore and the gold are as one.

Still falls the Rain —
Still falls the Blood from the Starved Man's wounded Side:
He bears in His Heart all wounds, — those of the light that died,
The last faint spark
In the self-murdered heart, the wounds of the sad uncompre-
    hending dark,

89

The wounds of the baited bear, —
The blind and weeping bear whom the keepers beat
On his helpless flesh . . . the tears of the hunted hare.

Still falls the Rain —
Then — O Ile leape up to my God: who pulles me doune —
See, see where Christ's blood streames in the firmament:
It flows from the Brow we nailed upon the tree
Deep to the dying, to the thirsting heart
That holds the fires of the world, — dark-smirched with pain
As Caesar's laurel crown.

Then sounds the voice of One who like the heart of man
Was once a child who among beasts has lain —
'Still do I love, still shed my innocent light, my Blood, for thee.'

Lullaby

THOUGH the world has slipped and gone,
Sounds my loud discordant cry
Like the steel birds' song on high:
'Still one thing is left — the Bone!'
Then out danced the Babioun.

She sat in the hollow of the sea —
A socket whence the eye's put out —
She sang to the child a lullaby
(The steel birds' nest was thereabout).

'Do, do, do, do —
Thy mother's hied to the vaster race:
The Pterodactyl made its nest
And laid a steel egg in her breast —

90

Under the Judas-coloured sun.
She'll work no more, nor dance, nor moan,
And I am come to take her place.
Do, do.

There's nothing left but earth's low bed —
(The Pterodactyl fouls its nest):
But steel wings fan thee to thy rest,
And wingless truth and larvae lie
And eyeless hope and handless fear —
All these for thee as toys are spread,
Do — do —

Red is the bed of Poland, Spain,
And thy mother's breast, who has grown wise
In that fouled nest. If she could rise,
Give birth again,

In wolfish pelt she'd hide thy bones
To shield thee from the world's long cold,
And down on all fours shouldst thou crawl
For thus from no height canst thou fall —
Do, do.

She'd give no hands: there's naught to hold
And naught to make: there's dust to sift,
But no food for the hands to lift.
Do, do.

Heed my ragged lullaby,
Fear not living, fear not chance;
All is equal — blindness, sight,
There is no depth, there is no height:
Do, do.

The Judas-coloured sun is gone,
And with the Ape thou art alone —
Do,
    Do.'

Serenade: Any Man to Any Woman

DARK angel who art clear and straight
As cannon shining in the air,
Your blackness doth invade my mind
And thunderous as the armoured wind
That rained on Europe is your hair;

And so I love you till I die —
(Unfaithful I, the cannon's mate):
Forgive my love of such brief span,
But fickle is the flesh of man,
And death's cold puts the passion out.

I'll woo you with a serenade —
The wolfish howls the starving made;
And lies shall be your canopy
To shield you from the freezing sky.

Yet when I clasp you in my arms —
Who are my sleep, the zero hour
That clothes, instead of flesh, my heart, —
You in my heaven have no part,
For you, my mirage broken in flower,

Can never see what dead men know!
Then die with me and be my love:
The grave shall be your shady grove
And in your pleasaunce rivers flow

(To ripen this new Paradise)
From a more universal Flood
Than Noah knew: but yours is blood.

Yet still you will imperfect be
That in my heart like death's chill grows,
— A rainbow shining in the night,
Born of my tears . . . your lips, the bright
Summer-old folly of the rose.

Street Song

'LOVE my heart for an hour but my bone for a day —
At least the skeleton smiles, for it has a morrow:
But the hearts of the young are now the dark treasure of Death,
And summer is lonely.

Comfort the lonely light and the sun in its sorrow,
Come like the night, for terrible is the sun
As truth, and the dying light shows only the skeleton's hunger
For peace, under the flesh like the summer rose.

Come through the darkness of death, as once through the
    branches
Of youth you came, through the shade like the flowering door
That leads into Paradise, far from the street, — you, the unborn
City seen by the homeless, the night of the poor.

You walk in the city ways, where Man's threatening shadow
Red-edged by the sun like Cain, has a changing shape —
Elegant like the Skeleton, crouched like the Tiger,
With the age-old wisdom and aptness of the Ape.

The pulse that beats in the heart is changed to the hammer
That sounds in the Potter's Field where they build a new world
From our Bone, and the carrion-bird days' foul droppings and
     clamour —
But you are my night, and my peace, —

The holy night of conception, of rest, the consoling
Darkness when all men are equal, — the wrong and the right,
And the rich and the poor are no longer separate nations, —
They are brothers in night.'

This was the song I heard; but the Bone is silent!
Who knows if the sound was that of the dead light calling, —
Of Caesar rolling onward his heart, that stone,
Or the burden of Atlas falling?

Song

ONCE my heart was a summer rose
That cares not for right or wrong,
And the sun was another rose, that year,
They shone, the sun and the rose, my dear —
Over the long and the light summer land
All the bright summer long.

As I walked in the long and the light summer land
All that I knew of shade
Was the cloud, my ombrelle of rustling grey
Sharp silk, it had spokes of grey steel rain —
Hiding my rose away, my dear,
Hiding my rose away.

And my laughter shone like a flight of birds
All in the summer gay, —
Tumbling pigeons and chattering starlings
And other pretty darlings, my dear,
And other pretty darlings.

To my heart like a rose, a rain of tears
(All the bright summer long)
Was only the sheen on a wood-dove's breast,
And sorrow only her song, my love —
And sorrow only my rest.

I passed a while in Feather Town —
(All the bright summer long) —
The idle wind puffed that town up
In air, then blew it down.

I walk alone now in Lead Town
(All in the summer gay . . .)
Where the steady people walk like the Dead —
And will not look my way.

For withering my heart, that summer rose,
Came another heart like a sun, —
And it drank all the dew from the rose, my love,
And the birds have forgotten their song
That sounded all summer long, my dear —
All the bright summer long.

The Song of the Cold

TO NATASHA LITVIN

HUGE is the sun of amethysts and rubies,
And in the purple perfumes of the polar sun
And homeless cold they wander.
But winter is the time for comfort, and for friendship,
For warmth and food —
And a talk beside a fire like the Midnight Sun, —
A glowing heart of amber and of musk. Time to forget
The falling night of the world and heart, the polar chaos
That separates us each from each. It is no time to roam
Along the pavements wide and cold as Hell's huge polar street,
Drifting along the city like the wind
Blowing aimlessly, and with no home
To rest in, only famine for a heart —
While Time means nothing to one, as to the wind
Who only cares for ending and beginning.

Here in the fashionable quarters of the city
Cold as the universal blackness of Hell's day
The two opposing brotherhoods are swept
Down the black marble pavements, Lethe's river.
First come the worlds of Misery, the small and tall Rag-Castles,
Shut off from every other. These have no name,
Nor friend to utter it . . . these of the extinct faces
Are a lost civilization, and have no possession
But the night and day, those centuries of cold.
Even their tears are changed now to the old
Eternal nights of ice round the loveless head
Of these who are lone and sexless as the Dead.

Dives of the Paleocrystic heart, behold
These who were once your brothers! Hear their voices
Hoarsened by want to the rusty voice of the tiger, no more
 crying
The death of the soul, but lamenting their destitution.
What life, what solar system of the heart
Could bring a restitution
To these who die of the cold?
       Some keep their youthful graces,
Yet in their winding-sheets of rags seem early
Made ready for the grave. . . . Worn to the bone by their
 famine
As if by the lusts that the poor Dead have known,
Who now are cold for ever. . . . Those who are old
Seem humbler, lean their mouths to the earth as if to crop
The kind earth's growth — for this is the Cainozoic period
When we must learn to walk with the gait of the Ape and Tiger:
The warmth of the heart is dead, or has changed to the world's
 fever —
And love is but masked murder, the lust for possession,
The hunger of the Ape, or the confession
Of the last fear, the wish to multiply
Their image, of a race on Oblivion's brink.

Lazarus, weep for those who have known the lesser deaths, O
 think
How we should pity the High Priests of the god of this world,
 the saints of Mammon,
The cult of gold! For see how these, too, ache with the cold
From the polar wastes of the heart. . . . See all they have given
Their god! Are not their veins grown ivy-old,
And have they not eaten their own hearts and lives in their
 famine?

Their huge Arithmetic is but the endless
Repetition of Zero — the unlimited,
Eternal. — Even the beat of the heart and the pulse is changed to
   this:
The counting of small deaths, the repetition
Of Nothing, endless positing and suppression of
                              Nothing. . . . So they live
And die of inanition. . . .
                      The miser Foscue
Weaving his own death and sinking like a spider
To vaults and depths that held his gold, that sun,
Was walled in that grave by the rotting hand of the dust, by a
   trap-door falling.
Do the enormous rays of that Sun now warm his blood, the
   appalling
Empty gulf of his veins — or fertilize
His flesh, that continent of dryness? . . . Yellow, cold,
And crumbling as his gold,
Deserted by the god of this world, a Gold Man like a terrible
   Sun,
A Mummy with a Lion's mane
He sits in this desert where no sound of wave shall come,
And Time's sands are of gold, filling his ears and eyes;
And he who has grown the talons of the Lion
Has devoured the flesh of his own hands and heart in his pain.

Pity these hopeless acolytes . . . the vain
Prudence that emulates the wisdom of the Spider
Who spins but for herself — a world of Hunger
Constructed for the needs of Hunger. . . . Soon
Their blankets will be thinner than her thread:
When comes the Night when they have only gold
For flesh, for warmth, for sheet —

O who would not pity these,
Grown fleshless too as those who starve and freeze!

Now falls the Night on Lazarus and Dives —
Those who were brothers, those who shared the pain
Of birth, and lusts, and the daily lesser deaths,
The beat of the dying heart, the careful breaths:
'You are so worn to the bone, I thought you were Death, my
   brother —
Death who will warm my heart.' 'Have you too known the cold?
Give me your hand to warm me. I am no more alone.
There was a sun that shone
On all alike, but the cold in the heart of Man
Has slain it. Where is it gone?'
So in the great Night that comes like love, so small they lie
As when they lay close to their mother's breast,
Naked and bare in their mortality.

Soon comes the Night when those who were never loved
Shall know the small immortal serpent's kiss
And turn to dust as lover turns to lover. . . .
Then all shall know the cold's equality. . . .
Young Beauty, bright as the tips of the budding vine,
You with the gold Appearances from Nothing rise
In the spring wind, and but for a moment shine.

Dust are the temples that were bright as heat . . .
And, perfumed nosegay brought for noseless Death,
Your brightest myrrh can not perfume his breath!

That old rag-picker blown along the street
Was once great Venus. But now Age unkind
Has shrunken her so feeble and so small —

Weak as a babe. And she who gave the Lion's kiss
Has now all Time's gap for her piteous mouth.
What lullaby will Death sing, seeing this
Small babe? And she of the golden feet,
To what love does she haste? After these centuries
The sun will be her only kiss — now she is blackened, shrunken,
   old
As the small worm — her kiss, like his, grown cold.

In the nights of spring, the inner leaf of the heart
Feels warm, and we will pray for the eternal cold
Of those who are only warmed by the sins of the world —
And those whose nights were violent like the buds
And roots of spring, but like the spring, grew old.
Their hearts are tombs on the heroic shore,
That were of iris, diamond, hyacinth,
And now are patterned only by Time's wave . . . the glittering
   plinth
Is crumbling. . . . But the great sins and fires break out of me
Like the terrible leaves from the bough in the violent spring . . .
I am a walking fire, I am all leaves —
I will cry to the Spring to give me the birds' and the serpents'
   speech
That I may weep for those who die of the cold —
The ultimate cold within the heart of Man.

Heart and Mind

SAID the Lion to the Lioness — 'When you are amber dust, —
No more a raging fire like the heat of the Sun
(No liking but all lust) —
Remember still the flowering of the amber blood and bone,
The rippling of bright muscles like a sea,
Remember the rose-prickles of bright paws
Though we shall mate no more
Till the fire of that sun the heart and the moon-cold bone are
    one.'

Said the Skeleton lying upon the sands of Time —
'The great gold planet that is the mourning heat of the Sun
Is greater than all gold, more powerful
Than the tawny body of a Lion that fire consumes
Like all that grows or leaps . . . so is the heart
More powerful than all dust. Once I was Hercules
Or Samson, strong as the pillars of the seas:
But the flames of the heart consumed me, and the mind
Is but a foolish wind.'

Said the Sun to the Moon — 'When you are but a lonely white
    crone,
And I, a dead King in my golden armour somewhere in a dark
    wood,
Remember only this of our hopeless love
That never till Time is done
Will the fire of the heart and the fire of the mind be one.'

Song

WE are the darkness in the heat of the day,
The rootless flowers in the air, the coolness: we are the water
Lying upon the leaves before Death, our sun,
And its vast heat has drunken us . . . Beauty's daughter
The heart of the rose and we are one.

We are the summer's children, the breath of evening, the days
When all may be hoped for, — we are the unreturning
Smile of the lost one, seen through the summer leaves —
That sun and its false light scorning.

Mary Stuart to James Bothwell

(Casket Letter No. II)

O YOU who are my heavenly pain of Hell,
My element, my Paradise of the First Man
That knows not sin — the eternity wherein I dwell!
Before the Flood were you not my primeval clay?
Did you not shape me from that chaos to the form
Of that which *men* call Murder — I, the light of the First Day?

Leaving you, I was sundered like the Sea!
Departed from the place where I left my heart
I was as small as any body may be
Whose heart is gone — small as the shade of Spring
That has no heart.
                    My mate, the leper-King,

White as a man of diamonds, spotted over
With the ermines of God's wrath for a kingly robe
— My leper-stick of bone

Covered with melting snows, to which I am crucified —
— Saw not Death gape wide
Wearing my smile, and bade me come again as his lover.

I was the thunder of the seas within man's blood, and the world's
    wonder!
But he sold my kiss for that of the fair-skinned Sickness
Who melted him away like the spring snows:
The bite of the bright-spotted leopard from Hell's thickets —
    this he chose!
She devoured his bones like fire . . . the bite that tore him
    asunder
Hidden behind the mouth of the ultimate Rose.

I lodged him in a beggar's house, Death-low
And ragged as a leper's flesh. . . . Then, weeping like the Spring
From amid his melting snow
He begged me watch by him, night long. Did I not know
His heart is wax,
While mine is diamond that no blow can break —
But only the touch of your hand, I had pitied those lidless eyes
    that must wake
Until Death seal them, mimicking my kiss.

But how should Pity stand between you and me!
The Devil sunder us from our mates, and God
Knit us together
Until nor man nor devil could tell lover from lover
In our heaven of damnation! Could these sunder our clay,

Or the seas of our blood? As well might they part the fires
That would burn to the bottom of Hell. . . . But there *is* no
   Hell —
We have kissed it away.

A Bird's Song

THE fire high up in air,
The bird, cries, 'I am the seed of fire
From the Sun — although I wear
A bird-mask. Now I swoop
Down to the archipelago of suns on the orange-tree in a dark
   sea of leaves.

O young Medea, fear
The sea in each fire that hangs upon your tree,
The cold in the heart of Man.
O guard that fleece of gold in your breast, your heart of fire;
Too soon it stolen will be!

Between smooth leaves where still the drops of night
Lie, the gold cold water-drops, I take my flight,
Shaking down the water-drops like the dark drowsy bees.
Beneath the orange-tree, the sleeper lies —
A bone of fire in a body of thin amber; the umbrageous tree
Has changed her to a bird of fire, feathered with shade, like me.

And I, the seed of the sun in a bird-mask,
Fly where from the perfumed stem and wind-smooth fruits
   down-pour

Such amber tears as the rich Sun doth weep
In his deep noonday sleep.'

In this deep night of leaves
And seas in a fire of gold,
If Man, the marauding faithless Jason, came, how should he
   know
Which is the gilded fleece and which the long and legendary
   Sea —
Which is the Sleeper's long and tangled hair and which the water-
   cold gold orange-tree?

The Shadow of Cain

TO C. M. BOWRA

UNDER great yellow flags and banners of the ancient Cold
Began the huge migrations
From some primeval disaster in the heart of Man.

There were great oscillations
Of temperature. . . . You knew there had once been warmth;

But the Cold is the highest mathematical Idea . . . the Cold is
   Zero —
The Nothing from which arose
All Being and all variation. . . . It is the sound too high for our
   hearing, the Point that flows

Till it becomes the line of Time . . . an endless positing
Of Nothing, or the Ideal that tries to burgeon
Into Reality through multiplying. Then Time froze

To immobility and changed to Space.
Black flags among the ice, blue rays
And the purple perfumes of the polar Sun
Freezing the bone to sapphire and to zircon —
These were our days.

And now in memory of great oscillations
Of temperature in that epoch of the Cold,
We found a continent of turquoise, vast as Asia
In the yellowing airs of the Cold: the tooth of a mammoth;
And there, in a gulf, a dark pine-sword

To show there had once been warmth and the gulf stream in our
    veins
Where only the Chaos of the Antarctic Pole
Or the peace of its atonic coldness reigns.
And sometimes we found the trace
Of a bird's claw in the immensity of the Cold:
The trace of the first letters we could not read:
Some message of Man's need,

And of the slow subsidence of a Race;
And of great heats in which the Pampean mud was formed,
In which the Megatherium Mylodon
Lies buried under Mastodon-trumpetings of leprous Suns.

The Earth had cloven in two in that primal disaster.
But when the glacial period began
There was still some method of communication

Between Man and his brother Man —
Although their speech
Was alien, each from each
As the Bird's from the Tiger's, born from the needs of our
    opposing famines.

Each said 'This is the Race of the Dead . . . their blood is
    cold. . . .
For the heat of those more recent on the Earth
Is higher . . . the blood-beat of the Bird more high
Than that of the ancient race of the primeval Tiger':
The Earth had lived without the Bird

In that Spring when there were no flowers like thunders in the
    air.
And now the Earth lies flat beneath the shade of an iron wing.
And of what does the Pterodactyl sing —
Of what red buds in what tremendous Spring?'

The thunders of the Spring began. . . . We came again
After that long migration
To the city built before the Flood by our brother Cain.
And when we reached an open door
The Fate said 'My feet ache'.
The Wanderers said 'Our hearts ache'.

There was great lightning
In flashes coming to us over the floor:
The Whiteness of the Bread —
The Whiteness of the Dead —
The Whiteness of the Claw —
All this coming to us in flashes through the open door.

There were great emerald thunders in the air
In the violent Spring, the thunders of the sap and the blood in
    the heart
— The Spiritual Light, the physical Revelation.

In the streets of the City of Cain there were great Rainbows
Of emeralds: the young people, crossing and meeting.

And everywhere
The great voice of the Sun in sap and bud
Fed from the heart of Being, the panic Power,
The sacred Fury, shouts of Eternity
To the blind eyes, the heat in the wingèd seed, the fire in the
    blood.

And through the works of Death,
The dust's aridity, is heard the sound
Of mounting saps like monstrous bull-voices of unseen fearful
    mimes:
And the great rolling world-wide thunders of that drumming
    underground

Proclaim our Christ, and roar 'Let there be harvest!
Let there be no more Poor —
For the Son of God is sowed in every furrow!'

We did not heed the cloud in the Heavens shaped like the hand
Of Man. . . . But there came a roar as if the Sun and Earth had
    come together —
The Sun descending and the Earth ascending
To take its place above . . . the Primal Matter
Was broken, the womb from which all life began.
Then to the murdered Sun a totem pole of dust arose in memory
    of Man.

The cataclysm of the Sun down-pouring
Seemed the roar
Of those vermilion Suns the drops of the blood
That bellowing like Mastodons at war
Rush down the length of the world — away — away —

The violence of torrents, cataracts, maelstroms, rains
That went before the Flood —
These covered the earth from the freshets of our brothers'
    veins;

And with them, the forked lightnings of the gold
From the split mountains,
Blasting their rivals, the young foolish wheat-ears
Amid those terrible rains.

The gulf that was torn across the world seemed as if the beds of
    all the Oceans
Were emptied. . . . Naked, and gaping at what once had been
    the Sun,
Like the mouth of the Universal Famine
It stretched its jaws from one end of the Earth to the other.

And in that hollow lay the body of our brother
Lazarus, upheaved from the world's tomb.
He lay in that great Death like the gold in the husk
Of the world . . . and round him, like spent lightnings, lay the
    Ore —
The balm for the world's sore.
And the gold lay in its husk of rough earth like the core
In the furred almond, the chestnut in its prickly
Bark, the walnut in a husk green and bitter.

And to that hollow sea
The civilization of the Maimed, and, too, Life's lepers, came
As once to Christ near the Sea of Galilee.

They brought the Aeons of Blindness and the Night
Of the World, crying to him, 'Lazarus, give us sight!
O you whose sores are of gold, who are the new Light
Of the World!'
                                    They brought to the Tomb
The Condemned of Man, who wear as stigmata from the womb
The depression of the skull as in the lesser
Beasts of Prey, the marks of Ape and Dog,
The canine and lemurine muscle . . . the pitiable, the terrible,
The loveless, whose deformities arose
Before their birth, or from a betrayal by the gold wheat-ear.
'Lazarus, for all love we knew the great Sun's kiss

On the loveless cheek. He came to the dog-fang and the lion-claw
That Famine gave the empty mouth, the workless hands.
He came to the inner leaf of the forsaken heart —
He spoke of our Christ, and of a golden love. . . .
But our Sun is gone . . . will your gold bring warmth to the
    loveless lips, and harvest to barren lands?'

Then Dives was brought. . . . He lay like a leprous Sun
That is covered with the sores of the world . . . the leprosy
Of gold encrusts the world that was his heart.
Like a great ear of wheat that is swoln with grain,
Then ruined by white rain,
He lay. . . . His hollow face, dust white, was cowled with a hood
    of gold:
But you saw there was no beat or pulse of blood —
You would not know him now from Lazarus!

He did not look at us.
He said 'What was spilt surges like the Flood.
But Gold shall be the Blood
Of the world. . . . Brute gold condensed to the primal essence
Has the texture, smell, warmth, colour of Blood. We must take

A quintessence of the disease for remedy. Once hold
The primal matter of all gold —
From which it grows
(That Rose of the World) as the sharp clear tree from the seed
    of the great rose,

Then give of this, condensed to the transparency
Of the beryl, the weight of twenty barley grains:
And the leper's face will be full as the rose's face
After great rains.

It will shape again the Shadow of Man. Or at least will take
From all roots of life the symptoms of the leper —
And make the body sharp as the honeycomb,
The roots of life that are left like the red roots of the rose-
    branches.'

But near him a gold sound —
The voice of an unborn wheat-ear accusing Dives —
Said 'Soon I shall be more rare, more precious than gold.'
There are no thunders, there are no fires, no suns, no earthquakes
Left in our blood. . . . But yet like the rolling thunders of all the
    fires in the world, we cry
To Dives: 'You are the shadow of Cain. Your shade is the
    primal Hunger.'
'I lie under what condemnation?'
'The same as Adam, the same as Cain, the same as Sodom, the
    same as Judas.

And the fires of your Hell shall not be quenched by the rain
From those torn and parti-coloured garments of Christ, those rags
That once were Men. Each wound, each stripe,
Cries out more loudly than the voice of Cain —
Saying "Am I my brother's keeper?"' Think! When the last
   clamour of the Bought and Sold
The agony of Gold
Is hushed. . . . When the last Judas-kiss
Has died upon the cheek of the Starved Man Christ, those ashes
   that were men
Will rise again
To be our Fires upon the Judgment Day!
And yet — who dreamed that Christ has died in vain?
He walks again on the Seas of Blood, He comes in the terrible
   Rain.

Bagatelle

FOR JOHN GIELGUD

Upon the soil — (crushed rubies? Or the pomegranate's garnet
   seeds?)
And ridged with mounds like graves
Of giants and earth-worms, two Noachian survivors contemplate
Their glories of the past, their future state.

The small red Worm, rubied with dews of Death, declared:
'My redness is from Adam. I, the coral-plant,
Built by a million lives, endeavours, toils, loves, glories,
Am the first and last Democracy. The sun

Is not more universal in its love. And I have brothers
Who live in the flesh of Negroes, and are thick
As lute-strings, and as powerful. I have others
Who sing the praise of Death with a sweet tongue —

Great venomous serpents in the unknown Africa; they carry
A gold bell on their tails, which ever ringeth
As they proceed, and like an angel singeth.'

Then said her enemy the Hen — the musty, dusty density,
The entity of primal, flightless, winged Stupidity:
'See how the Eagle falls like thunder from his height
And tears that continent of raging fire,
The heart, from the Tiger roaring like the sea,
And bears it to his nest
Wherein the huge eggs rest
From whence will break the young, the unfledged Murders:

(So, young ambitions lie in the heart of Man).
O you into whose maw
The heart of Man will fall
As you will fall to mine:
I am more powerful than the father of those Murders.

It was no Eagle, but a fusty Hen
That pecked the fire-seeds from Prometheus' heart, a crazy
    chilling
Hen-coop Laughter, the first Criticism, killing
The fire he brought to men,
As Age kills young Desire.'

The Worm said, 'I am small, my redness is from Adam.
But conquerors tall

113

Come to my embrace as I were Venus. I
Am the paramour in the last bed of love, and mine, the kiss
That gives Eternity.
I am Princess of Darkness. Yet the huge gold world,
With all plantations, powers of gold growth that shall be the
  bread of man,
Arise from the toil of the small, the mighty Worm beneath the
  earth —
The blind, all-seeing Power at her great work of death and of
  rebirth.'

THE ROAD TO THEBES—I

TO HUMPHREY AND GILLEN SEARLE

*Is the road from Thebes to Athens and the
road from Athens to Thebes the same?*
ARISTOTLE: *Physica*

Beside the Yellow Foam that Sings of
Lydian Airs

BESIDE the yellow foam that sings of Lydian airs and of the
  lyre —
And vines taut as the lyre the earth seems of sardonyx
Where the hot juices fall like yellow planets — earth striped
  like the lynx.

Along the road to Thebes
All polished speeds,
Men, horses, seeds,
Are blown by the bright wind, the young flute-player,
Who kindles every vine-bough, sharp
As shrill spring lightnings.
                              But what golden speed
Now lies beneath the earth, like the soul maimed
By the rough centaur-husk? For in the Pliocene
Strata lies the Horse,
The Pliohippus and Hipparion
Whose skin shone like the Pleiades — once fleet as the spring rain,
Or young desire, were they — as quickly gone.
Yet still the sound of waves and the long-dying
Airs and the great veils and veins and voices
Of vines are theirs,

The thunders of the bull-voiced mimes, unseen, unknown,
The thunders of saps rising, and of all things sown

In far-off gardens.
                        Ghosts rise from gold seeds
In the mist from vine-branches. 'And were you Agamemnon
Or the shrill ghost of a vine-tendril?' 'Should I know?'

I only know my form
Is the great logic of the winter, the geometry
Of Death: the world began with these:
The numbers of Pythagoras,
The seeds of Anaxagoras:
And the winter at my heart, whose Zero is
An infinite intensity, yet holds
The seeds and beginning of the fires of spring.

Now for the sound of wars, I hear bees among vine-blooms
Singing of growth — they, yellow as the planets,
Like Capricornus, Lynx, and Taurus swarming.

The Dead Man, thin as water,
Or as a vine-tendril, and shod with gold
As for a journey — (but upon what road?) —

Answered the thunders of the saps rising
Under the dust thàt shines like the glittering skin
Of centaurs in horse-bearing Thessaly:

'Is your gold-sinewed body still a vine-branch
In the vineyards of great Venus?' 'Shrunk to this
Poor span, I have returned to the likeness of the first and final
    Worm that is my brother:
For were we not born of the same holy mother —

Alike in holiness? . . . Now black as earth.
Yet great queens found my mouth
As a dark leaf of nardus brought from Syria —
Of the gold door of the South.
                         Ah, who
Would kiss it now?
                    And those queens' dust is but as
    frost that shines like fire
Or the gilded dust of Venus in the spring,
Fertilizing the crocus.

                    As I went on my long road
From Birth to Death, I learned that Birth and Death,
The road to Thebes from Athens, and the road

116

From Thebes to Athens, coming and going, praise and blame,
Are like the angry kings, the ghosts of gold
That hide from Man his sun: they are the same.

Upon my road from Birth to Death, to Thebes from Athens,
I heaped gold dust in hills.
                                    With the blind mole,
On my returning way, I heaped another mound
Of dust. And as I came

On my Night-Road, the four gigantic thunders sounded:
And the four worlds were gone: Earth, Water, Fire and Air.
With Death, in nakedness, I was alone:
But then heard the great thunders of saps rising and of all things
    sown.

The four worlds came: Love, Hate, Belief and Unbelief:
The raging human dust, dull dust of brutes,
The groping dust of plants, the earth's blind dust).
On my Day Road, the four gigantic thunders sounded:
The worlds fell from the living heart, were gone,
And I was alone with Life — the Naked Man.

The worlds went: I was a clod of earth
Blown by the wind along the road from Death to Birth.
The worlds came: I was clothed with a little dust,
And blown along the road from Birth to Death.

I cried at the light, as I had cried at the dark.
I found a little rest upon my way, a small child growing
Deep in the tomb, or in my mother's womb —
But still unknowing.

In my canicular days, I, the companion
Of the high Sun, could never dream of setting,
Or that I should not find the answer to the Question.'

.   .   .   .

There was no sign of the lion-bodied one
Between the vineyards and the heroic sea,
There was no glitter of her mane, strong as the wave,
Bright as the treasure on the ocean-floor,
And the glittering orange-tree. There was no sound

Where the lion-coloured dusts are numerous as Time's sands,
Under the heavens masked with gold like Agamemnon,

And bordered with great vines whose solar system of the
   grapes
Shines like the centaur's skin, hard as cornelian grains,
The hue of honey sarcophagizing or of sard —
Holding small stars for seeds
And planets of noon-dew, and the long rains
And the cool sea-winds from the far horizons.

As I went my way from the cities of the living
Dead to cities of the dead Living, airs and prayers
Arose from the fertility of vines,
From cornucopias and corruptions, continents
Of growth, from where those seeds, the Dead, are sown
To be reborn, and germs of evil that exist in Matter
Are changed by holy earth, to the common good,

To usefulness, fertility. The breath
Of the Ardent Belief, of the cultivated earth

Drifts through the city streets, to kings turned dust-worms,
To beggars and bugbears, dusty thunders, Cerberus
Changed to a dog, and Niobe to a stone lest she should weep —

To palaces of Commerce, the machine, the revolutions
Rushing toward the vortices (gyrations
Of empty Light), and Man, like Ixion, bound
Upon that wheel, all in the conquering dust;
To palaces of Justice — a projection of the Darkness:
(Domitian, the mad Emperor, catching flies, and Harcateus,
The King of Parthia, a blind mole-catcher) —

To Afternoon-Men, Giddy-heads, the chrysalides,
The Golden Outsides, drones, flies, and philosophers,
A world of busy sleep
Where the horse drives the man, the palace builds
The slave, the judge the criminal, and the sun gilds

Laughing and weeping, hatred, fear, and love, and lust
With royal robes, soon to be changed to dust.

Then comes the hour of consolation, and the evening,
Sighing all sighs and knowing all ambitions, walks like the wave
To cities whose names are like the sound of waves, Aomono,
Quezaltenango, Wawasee, Tandora,
London and Paris.

A sound drifts through the streets to the
homeward-going —
A golden dust — from the evening? From the hives of Midas?
From the Lion-gate?
Or the sands of Time whence the Lion-bodied asks the Question
On roads sacred to Man, who is great as a planet moving
On its gold tendril, — small as a grain of dust.

The Night Wind

O HEART, great equinox of the Sun of Night
Where life and death are equal — Lion — or Sphinx!
What can you tell of Darkness
To the great continent of hungry stone?

Heart, (Lion or Sphinx) what can you tell the city
Of breasts like Egypt where no lightning shines,
Because of their great heat? This is the hour the night-wind
Asks those born in Hell concerning their foredoom.

Now in the streets great airs the colour of the vines
Drift to the noctuas, veiled women, to the faceless ones, the
    nameless ones —
To Lot's wife staring across the desert of her life.

Those airs of sapphire drift from violet vines —
Elixirs and saps of sapphire beloved of Saturn,
And planets of violet dew from vine-branches

Fall on the lips of fashionable women —
The abominable Koretto and Metro (cities buried
Under the sands of the Dead Sea: Adama and Gomorrah, Segor);
And cool the cheeks where the long fires of all Hell are dyed;

Drifting to women like great vines: (what was the first plantation
    since the Flood?
The vines of Grief?

The first sin of the new world, and the last
Of the ancient civilization? You, the night-wind,
What was the first plantation since the Flood?)

And to old Maenads of the city, where the far-off music,
Dying in public gardens, wraps their flesh —
That vast immundity from which the Flood receded,
Their hearts, those rocks from which no Moses could strike tears,

With a little comfort; they, awhile forgetting
The mobilization of the world's filth, the garrets, garners
Of Nothingness, and the sparse fire's infrequent garnets,
The ragpicker's great reign, their empty mouths like Chaos
    ruined,
Speak for a moment with their other lives:

'What is it knocks at that tomb my heart? Is it the grave-digger,
The final Adam? There was one knocked so:
He would not know me now. For all Time's filth, the dress
I stole from the habitations of the Dead,
Hides me — a body cold as the wind-blown vines,
And the sad sapphire bone shrunk by Time's fires

To this small apeish thing.'
                              'Ah, what was I inferior to Death
That you should be untrue? Now, kindly Age,
My one companion, holds me close, so I
Forget your kiss. The fires in my heart are gone.
And yet, as if they had melted into rain,

The heart itself, my tears
Are faithful yet.'

            'Is there another language of the Dead?
Is that why those for whom we long return
No more? For the small words of love they say —

How should we hear them through the Babel-clamour?
They make no sound:
All the great movements of the world pass with no noise:
The golden boys,
The great Spring, turn to dust as to a lover —
The heart breaks with no sound.'

'And in the day, the empire of hatred and of hunger,
Even the Dog pities us! "I would be destitute as Man,
So cast from me my faithfulness, my one possession.
All day, my throat must multiply its thunder
To the triple violence of Cerberus
To proclaim your misery and mine! Why should the Beast and
    Reptile
Be imprisoned in their small empire of aggression —
The claw, fang, sting, the twining, the embrace?"
Has Man no more than this? Does not the lover say to lover:
"Is that your kiss?

It is more cold than the python, the shining one, the viper;
Its venom is perfidy, outshining all the stars."'

Then where the suns of Night seek in the rock for unborn
    sapphires
And cornflowers like blue flames or water-drops from wells of
    blue fire
Deep as the heart of Man, from which to build the Day,

I went upon my road to Thebes from Athens, Death from Birth,
And to my heart, that last dark Night in which the long Styx
    weeps its woe,
Held close the world, my wound.

Song

You said, 'This is the time of the wild spring'

FOR ROY AND MARY CAMPBELL

YOU said, 'This is the time of the wild spring and the mating of
    the tigers,
This is the first vintage of the heat like the budding of wild
    vines —
The budding of emeralds and the emerald climate,

When flowers change into rainbows and young insects
Are happy, the people have heart-strings like the music
Of the great suns, oh never to be quenched by darkness.'

But I am the water-carrier to the Damned, and dark as water.
Only those nights, my eyes, have no more rain,
And dead are the merciful fountains
Since the world changed into a stone again.

I am the grave of the unpitied Sisyphus,
My heart, that rolled the universe, a stone
Changed to me, like your heart, up endless mountains.

The Blinded Song-Bird near the Battle-Field

TO C. W. MCCANN

HERE, in the terrible Butterfly-climate of this world
Where the Stigmata is changed to the sign of the Feather —

I sit within my cage, am blind as the world.
Once I was Daedalus
And flew too near the sun. But in my fall

Brought back a feather from those thunderous wings for song —
To comfort my world's darkness, the world's wrong.
And now one goldfinch light
Sings 'Happy are you that you have no sight!'

For as I flew, I saw upon the earth
One limbless, eyeless, as before his birth, —
And torn by all the nails upon Christ's Cross:
He bore the Stigmata of the sins of the whole world.

And from the little span
Of his heart fell the blood — the sea of Galilee
Whereon Christ walked . . . that ghost of Abel whispers o'er
    the world:
'Brother, I come.
I have no eyes
But my all-seeing wounds; and I am dumb,
But yet from all the open mouths of the world's wounds I rise:
I come to testify.'

Sailor, What of the Isles?

TO MILLICENT HUDDLESTON ROGERS

'SAILOR, what of the isles —
The green worlds grown
From a little seed? What of the islands known and those un-
  known?'

'I have returned over the long and lonely sea;
And only human need
For the world of men is mine; I have forgot Immensity.

The rustling sea was a green world of leaves;
The isle of Hispaniola in its form
Was like the leaf of a chestnut tree in June.
And there is the gold region — the gold falls like rain with a
  long and leafy tune.

An old man bore us lumps of gold . . . the small,
Like walnuts husked with earth; the great,
As large as oranges, and leafy earth
Still clung to them. And when you thought that fireflies lit the
  night,
These were but nuggets, lying on the dark earth, burning
  bright.'

'Sailor, what of the maps of the known world?' 'The old
  Chinese,
Whose talk was like the sound of June leaves drinking rain,
Constructed maps of the known world — the few
Islands and two countries that they knew.

They thought the heavens were round,
The earth square, and their empire at the earth's centre . . .
                    just as you
And I believe we are the world's centre and the stars
Are grown from us as the bright seas in a rind of gold
Are grown from the smooth stem of the orange-tree.

Those maps of the Yellow Empire then were drawn,
As we think, upside down:
Tongking was placed
Where usually the North stands, and Mongolia graced
The South. The names, too, were writ upside down.
For how is it possible, in this flat world, to know
Why South should be below, the North above —
Why man should hold creeds high one moment, the next
    moment low?'

'Sailor, what of the maps of skies? Is that Orion?'
                                        'No, the sight
Is of a far island. What you see
Is where they are gathering carbuncles, garnets, diamonds bright
As fireflies with a gardener's rake under the spice-trees and the
    orange-trees.'

'Sailor, what do you know of this world, my Self . . . a child
Standing before you? — Or an isle
To which no sail has crossed over the long and lonely sea?
What do you know of this island, of the soil
In which all sainthood or insanity, murder or mockery grows —
    leafy tree?'

'No more than the gardeners and astronomers who make
Their catalogues of stars for heavens and seeds for garden beds

Know of their green worlds; or the soil, of the great beasts
Whose skin shines like gold fire or fireflies, and whose nostrils
    snort great stars —
The beasts — huge flowers grown from the stem of the green
    darkness; each beast holds
The entire world of plants,
All elements and all the planetary system in
Itself (while the flower holds only the plant-world)
And freed from its stem by light, like the flowers in air —

No more than the father knows of the child, or the sailor of
    chartless isles.'

The Queen of Scotland's Reply to a Reproof from John Knox

FOR GORDON WATSON

SAID the bitter Man of Thorns to me, the White Rose-Tree:
'That wonted love of yours is but an ass's bray —
The beast who called to beast
And kicked the world away!'
(All the wisdom of great Solomon
Held in an ass's bray.)

When body to body, soul to soul
Were bare in the fire of night
As body to grave, as spirit to Heaven or Hell,
What did we say?

'Ah, too soon we shall be air —
No pleasure, anguish, will be possible.
Hold back the day!'
For in this moment of the ass-furred night
You called the hour of the Beast, was born
All the wisdom of great Solomon
From the despisèd clay!
All the wisdom of Solomon
Held in an ass's bray.

TWO RAW SONGS OF JACK STRAW

TO L. P. HARTLEY

1. The Death of Prometheus

OUTSIDE the wall
Of the death-room where the tall
Prometheus lay,
As grey as a boxing kangaroo Eternity's sea is fighting
A yawning ghost — a ghost with a donkey's bray:
'Hee-haw!
See-saw!
Now up, now down,
Now King, now Clown!
I am the new Equality, mine is the day.'
No Furies watch, for in their place are flies
Who with the beating of dark wings are finding
The world's new rhythm (a little buzzing in air, then silence),
In which the Giant and Dwarf take it in turns

To rule: Up Giant! Down Dwarf! Up Dwarf!
Down Giant! Thin as Man's faith, or the Writing on the Wall,
The teachers laugh (Jim No-one, small Joe None,
Jack Straw and John Raw),
And Man is alone.
'Not much of a world to leave!' Prometheus said.
Then, as world-long he lay on his death-bed,
With the marrow of his bone, his brain, clean-eaten
By those who were his friends, the great fires beaten
To ash from the Burning Bush that was his heart,
His Will was read to those friends. No deserts hold
Beasts more desperate — horses pretending to be men,
And riding men for horses, foxes, jackals,
Hiding behind their human faces. Bold,
The little Jackal with his gilded pelt
(Hiding the leprous spot and the world's rot)
Giggles, 'No more need I know the Lion's weather —
But a time to sprawl and to wear the Ape's feather!
I shall boast of the Lion's kill as my own,
And shall build my castle of the Lion's bone!'
And with that all the animals hell-howled together,
With yawning mouth's like Time's, into whose maw
In the end all Caesars, cities, suns,
Will in their ruin fall
With the old bacchantes of the suburbs and the red
Lilies named Cynorrhodon — yet more
Voracious. But the Giant's Will said,
'My loving friends, on my life you have richly fed.
But now you have eaten me bare to the heart and bone,
You must look to One you starved in your greed —
Not the see-saw world (there is no world left, all is loss).
There is only the echo that quenches the thirst in Hell —
The sound of the terrible tears that will fall from the Cross.'

2. At the Crossroads

THE Beast of Prey has not a history —
A blaring backward shadow of despair
Or triumph — only the shadow of the Lion's paw
Across the world, foretelling the new Law.

In the month of mellow August, of the auguries
Of dust, and yellow moons and melons, shadows
Yellow as the ripeness and the wheat
Fall in the great heat
On crossroads of the world, where Man must make
The choice — of the backward road to the Peaceful Ape,
Or the forward road to the company of the Lion
That has no backward history, but only
The long predestination of the Lion's paw.

Where the crossroads meet, the toppling gods of straw,
Gapus, Vervactoris, Convectoris,
Imporcitoris (nodding at John Raw
And Niny-Nany: Man pretending to be real)
Whine: 'We are wheat' to the grave's mocking maw.
One creaks:
'Man follows our rocking law —
Changed by each hollow breeze.' Convectoris said,
'Ripeness is all!

And Man's whole duty is to find the quickest way to fall.
You, King and Beggar, who in the womb wore the Ape's coat,
The lanugo, should learn in the Ape's school
To walk on all fours, cast a longer shade to cool
The world — you who are now but shade!' Another teacher said,

'If Man rejects the religion of the Straw,
The Lion will blot out History — The paw
Of the Lion who finds its nourishment in Man's bones
That have grown dry as the bones of Tantalus
From thirst of gold, this will erase
The scarlet dawns of History in the veins. . . .
Darkness is all.'
So sounds the Fool's song, as he sees our planet cool.

'His Blood Colours My Cheek'
A saying of St. Agnes

FOR THE VERY REV. M. C. D'ARCY, S.J., LL.D.,
D.LITT., LITT.D., F.R.S.L.

His Blood colours my cheek.
Ah! Were but those Flames the tongue wherewith I speak
Of the small ambitions I have seen
Rise in the common street
Where the bell that tolls in Bedlam tolls the hour.
Yet still great flowers like violet thunders break
In air, and still the flower of the five-petalled senses
Is surely ours.
I, an old dying woman, tied
To the winter's hopelessness
And to a wisp of bone
Clothed in the old world's outworn foolishness
— A poor Ape-cerement
With all its rags of songs, loves, rages, lusts, and flags of death,

Say this to you,
My father Pithecanthropus Erectus, your head once filled with
  primal night,
You who stood at last after the long centuries
Of the anguish of the bone
Reaching upward towards the loving, the all-understanding
  sun —
To you, who no more walk on all fours like the first
Gardener and grave-digger, yet are listening
Where, born from zero, little childish leaves and lives begin!
I hear from the dust the small ambitions rise.
The White Ant whispers: 'Could I be Man's size,

My cylinders would stretch three hundred feet
In air, and Man would look at me with different eyes!'
And there the Brazilian insect all day long
Challenges the heat with its heavy noise:
'Were I as great as Man, my puny voice
Would stretch from Pole to Pole, no other sound
Be audible. By this dictatorship the round
World would be challenged — from my uproar would a new
Civilization of the dust be born, the old world die like dew.'
I watch the new world of rulers, the snub-nosed, the vain and
  the four-handed,
Building a new Babel for the weak
Who walk with the certainty of the somnambulist
Upon the tight-rope stretched over nothingness —
Holding a comet and the small ape-dust in their fist
Over the grave where the heart of Man is laid.
I hear the empty straw whine to the street
Of the ghost that has no bread, the lonely ghost
That lacks prosperity: 'I am your Wheat:
Come and be fed!'

But I see the sun, large as the journeying foot of Man, see the
  great traveller
Fearing no setting, going straight to his destination,
So am I not dismayed.
His Blood colours my cheek; —
No more eroded by the seas of the world's passions and greeds,
  I rise
As if I never had been ape, to look in the compassionate, the all-
  seeing Eyes.

A Girl's Song in Winter

FOR CYRIL CONNOLLY

THAT lovely dying white swan the singing sun
Will soon be gone. But seeing the snow falling, who could tell
  one
From the other? The snow, that swan-plumaged circling crea-
  ture, said,
'Young girl, soon the tracing of Time's bird-feet and the bird-
  feet of snow
Will be seen upon your smooth cheek. Oh, soon you will be
Colder, my sweet, than me!'

La Bella Bona Roba

FOR HAROLD ACTON

I cannot tell who loves the skeleton
Of a poor marmoset, nought but boan, boan,
Give me a nakednesse with her cloaths on.
                    RICHARD LOVELACE

ALAS, lass, lost —
Alas, lost.

Where is my white velvet dress
Of flesh that some called heaven, some sin —
Not pitying the grave that is
Not slaked, that is not satisfied,
For all its triumph? Ah, lass, lost!
Alas, lost.

My arms were mighty as the seas
That gird the great young seeding lands
To make them theirs, and in my hands
Men's fortunes were as Time's sand in
The glass . . . I gave them at the last
The small red worm for paramour.
Where is that might now? Ah, lass, lost!
Alas, all lost.

Once my love had the lion's mouth,
My breasts were the pillars of the South.
Now my mouth has the desert's drouth,

And all that comes
To my breast is the wind and rain —
Alas, lass, lost,
Alas, lost.

The tigerish Spring was in each vein;
The glittering wind of Spring, my mane.
Now am I no more to Spring
Than the violet mist from vine-branches.
Alas, lass, lost.
All, lass, lost.

Now is my body only this:
The infinite geometry
That is the cold. How could I know
Winter would take me, I grow old?
Alas, lass, lost.
Alas, lost.

Young girl, you stare at me as if
I were that Medusa Time
That will change you, too, to stone:
So you, grown old, must lie alone.
Alas, lass, lost!
Alas. . . .

The Yellow Girl

FOR ALBERTO DE LACERDA

In this island [Hispaniola] are certain glow worms that shine in the night, as doe ours . . . but give a greater light, so much that when the men of the Iland goe any journeys in the night, they beare some of these wormes made fast about their feet and head, in such sort that he should see them afarre. By the light of these also, the women worke in their houses in the night.

GONZALO DE ORVIEDO

ONCE the Reverend Thomas Glover,
In the prow of his boat drifting
O'er a sea as clear as tropic
Air, read from the Holy Book
By the light of a small worm.
(All the heavens and God's fire
Revealed through a small worm's desire.)

A skeleton lying on the sand
(Like the gold-dark skeleton of the sun)
That ship-wrecked sailor sighing said:

'The leaf-dark King of Aragon
Sent me as Ambassador
To the Sultan of Great Babylon
Over the sea (a world of leaves)
But I was wrecked upon Time's sands
And in the isle of My Yellow Girl
I died of the Yellow Fever, O!

For she was brighter than the gold
That falls from the leaves of Hispaniola;
A bouquet of the yellow stars,

Her mouth . . . Her voice like moonlight, or
The voice of the sea-sorrow, told
Me "Wander not — I love thee!" So
I slept with that yellow moonlight, and
I died of the Yellow Fever, O!
Some men turn skeletons for gold,
And some for love of the horizons;
Or because Truth, a water-lady
As inconstant as the wave,
Rose from the depths of the tropic sea
And lured them to her siren cave.
But at the last, all things are one:
Gold, Truth and the skeleton of the sun
When we alone are lying.

My girl was lovely as Idleness,
But Shadow now, the giantess,
(Dark Africa as calm as palm trees) is
My sole companion.
Grave sir, you preach with book and bell
Against the Yellow Girl, the moonlight
I had thought was day . . .
And yet, despise not the poor clay:
Do you not read the Holy Book
By the despisèd small worm's light —
All the heavens and God's Fire
All the Spirit's storm
Revealed through a small worm's desire?'

Praise We Great Men

FOR BENJAMIN BRITTEN

PRAISE we great men
From all the hearths and homes of men, from hives
Of honey-making lives.
Praise with our music those
Who bring the morning light
To the hearts of men, those households of high heaven, Praise

We those gods of sound
Who stole the frozen fire
From gilded hives upon Mount Parnassus,
(Hives gilded by the light) — compressed
That honey-red fire into holy forms
That emulate those of the hives of heaven. Praise

Those who can raise
Gold spirits of men from their rough Ape-dust, and who see
The glory, grandeur hidden in small forms:
The planetary system in the atom, and great suns
Hid in a speck of dust. Praise we the just —

Who are not come to judge, but bless
Immortal things in their poor mortal dress,

And ripen lives and rule our hearts and rhythms,
Immortal hungers in the veins and heart.

Praise be to those who sing
Green hymns of the great waters to the dry

And tearless deserts in the souls of men, until
Under the fertilization of their singing breath
Even the greyness and the dust of Death
Seem the grey pollen of the long September heat. O, praise
With lion-music such as that heard in the air
When the roaring golden lion that roams the heavens
Devours the dark, and multitudes and magnitudes respond

To that lion-music. . . . And on wings
Of music let us rise
Like velvet honey-flies
To praise the gods of sound with those bee-murmurings:

The sound of violins
And the clear sound of flutes
As round as honeyed fruits —
(And like the water-Phoenix ever rising
For wanderers in the lonely desert sand —)

Praise we these earthly gods —
Praise with the trumpet's purple sound —
Praise with the trumpet flower
And with that flower the long five-petalled hand
That sweeps the strings.
Praise with that Angel of High God the voice —
O let us still rejoice
And praise we these great men from the first hour
Of the spirit's birth until our earthly setting

Into the night of Death.
Praise with our last breath
These earthly Gods who bring

All sounds, all faiths, delights and splendours lost
Beneath the winter's frost
Back to the hearts, the hearths and homes of men.

Fires on the hearth, fires in the skies, fires in the human heart,
Praise we great men!

NOTES

JODELLING SONG

(Page 48)

THIS is founded on Gertrude Stein's 'Accents in Alsace' (The Watch on the Rhine) contained in her book *Geography and Plays*:

'Sweeter than water or cream or ice. Sweeter than bells of roses. Sweeter than winter or summer or spring. Sweeter than pretty posies. Sweeter than anything is my queen and loving is her nature.

'Loving and good and delighted and best is her little King and Sire whose devotion is entire, who has but one desire to express the love which is hers to inspire.

'In the photograph the Rhine hardly showed.

'In what way do chimes remind you of singing? In what ways do birds sing? In what way are forests black or white?

'We saw them blue.

'With forget-me-nots.

'In the midst of our happiness we were very pleased.'

GOLD COAST CUSTOMS

(Page 60)

'The Negroes indulge that perfect contempt for humanity which in its bearing on Justice and Morality is the fundamental characteristic of the race. They have, moreover, no knowlede of the immortality of the soul, although spectres are supposed to appear. The undervaluing of humanity among them reaches an incredible degree of intensity. Tyranny is regarded as no wrong, and cannibalism is looked upon as quite customary and proper. Among us instinct deters from it, if we can speak of instinct at all as appertaining to man. But with the Negro this is not the case, and the devouring of human flesh is altogether consonant with the general principles of the African race; to the sensual Negro, human flesh is but an object of sense — mere flesh. At the death of a king hundreds are killed and eaten; prisoners are butchered and their flesh sold in the market-place; the victor is accustomed to eat the flesh of his fallen foe.' — Hegel, *Philosophy of History*.

It is needless to add that this refers only to a past age, and that, in quoting this passage, I intend no reflection whatever upon the African races of our time. This passage no more casts a reflection upon them than a passage referring to the cruelties of the Tudor age casts a reflection upon the English of our present age. — E. S.

(Page 60, line 5)

'Munza rattles his bones in the dust.' King Munza reigned, in 1874, over the Monbuttoo, a race of cannibals in Central Africa. These notes are taken from Dr. George Schweinfurth's *The Heart of Africa* (translated by Ellen Frewer, published by Messrs. Sampson Low). Of the Monbuttoo and their neighbours the Niam-Niam, we read: 'Human fat is universally sold. . . . Should any lone and solitary individual die, uncared for . . . he would be sure to be devoured in the very district in which he lived. During our residence at the Court of Munza the general rumour was quite current that nearly every day some little child was sacrificed to supply his meal. There are cases in which bearers who died from fatigue had been dug out of the graves in which they had been buried . . . in order that they might be devoured. The cannibalism of the Monbuttoo is the most pronounced of all the known nations of Africa. Surrounded as they are by a number of people who, being inferior to them in culture, are consequently held in great contempt, they have just the opportunity which they want for carrying on expeditions of war and plunder, which result in the acquisition of a booty which is especially coveted by them, consisting of human flesh. But with it all, the Monbuttoos are a noble race of men, men who display a certain national pride . . . men to whom one may put a reasonable question and receive a reasonable answer. The Nubians can never say enough in praise of their faithfulness in friendly intercourse and of the order and stability of their national life. According to the Nubians, too, the Monbuttoos were their superiors in the arts of war.'

(*Page* 65, *lines* 26 and 27)

'And her soul, the cannibal Amazon's mart.'

'Tradition alleges that in former times a state composed of women made itself famous by its conquests: it was a state at whose head was a woman. She is said to have pounded her son in a mortar, and to have had the blood of pounded children constantly at hand. She is said to have driven away or put to death all the males, and commanded the death of all male children. These furies destroyed everything in the neighbourhood, and were driven to constant plunderings because they did not cultivate the land. . . . This infamous state, the report goes on to say, subsequently disappeared.' — Hegel, *Philosophy of History*, chapter on Africa.

INVOCATION

(*Page* 81, *lines* 7 to 11)

'The blood, when present in the veins as part of a body, a generative part, too, and endowed with soul, being the soul's immediate instrument, and primary seat . . . the blood, seeming also to have a share of another divine body and being suffused with divine animal heat, suddenly acquires remarkable and most excellent powers, and is analogous to the essence of the stars. In so far as it is spirit, it is the hearth, the Vesta, the household divinity, the innate heat, the sun of the microcosm, the fire of Plato; not because like common fire it lightens, burns, and destroys, but because, by a vague and incessant motion, it preserves, nourishes, and aggrandizes itself. It further deserves the name of spirit, inasmuch as it is radical moisture, at once the ultimate and the proximate and the primary aliment.' — William Harvey (*The Works of William Harvey, M.D.*, translated from the Latin by R. Willis, Sydenham Society, 1847).

EURYDICE

(*Page* 85, *line* 31)

'. . . A most sweet wife, a young wife, *Nondum sustulerat flavum Proserpina crinem* (not yet had Proserpina tied up her golden hair) — such a

143

wife as no man ever had, so good a wife, but she is now dead and gone, *Lethaeoque jacet condita sarcophago* (she lies buried in the silent tomb).' — Robert Burton, *The Anatomy of Melancholy*.

(Page 87, lines 6 and 7)

'The light which God is shines in darkness, God is the true light: to see it one has to be blind and strip God naked of things.' — Meister Eckhart, *Sermons and Collations*, XIX.

(Page 88, lines 9 and 10)

> 'And her deadness
> Was filling her with fullness
> Full as a fruit with sweetness and darkness
> Was she with her great death.'
> — R. M. Rilke (translated J. B. Leishman).

LULLABY

(Page 90, line 5)

The phrase 'out-dance the Babioun' occurs in an Epigram by Ben Jonson.

THE SONG OF THE COLD

(Page 96, line 2)

'There was the morning when, with Her, you struggled amongst those banks of snow, those green-lipped crevasses, that ice, those black flags and blue rays, and purple perfumes of the polar sun. . . .' — Arthur Rimbaud, *Metropolitan* (translated by Helen Rootham).

(Page 96, lines 6 and 7)

'This evening, Devotion to Circeto of the tall mirrors, fat as a fish and glowing like the ten months of the red night (her heart is of amber

and musk) — for me a prayer, mute as those regions of night. . . .'
— Arthur Rimbaud, *Devotion*.

(*Page* 98, *line* 7)

The miser Foscue, a farmer-general of France, existing in Languedoc about 1760. These lines tell his actual story.

MARY STUART TO JAMES BOTHWELL
(*Casket Letter No. II*)
(*Page* 102)

This is the actual story of the Second Casket Letter, used as proof that Mary was guilty of complicity in the murder of Darnley.

(*Page* 102, *lines* 8 and 9)

A transcript of words ascribed to Mary.

(*Page* 102, *line* 12)

Darnley was known as 'the leper-King'. Towards the end of his life, he suffered from a disease which necessitated the hiding of his face behind a taffeta mask. This disease was ascribed by Mary's enemies to the result of poison, by her friends to the result of Darnley's excesses.

(*Page* 103, *line* 13)

It was a complaint against Mary that she lodged Darnley, at Kirk o' Field, the place of his death, in 'a beggarly house'.

(*Page* 103, *lines* 16 to 18)

A transcript of the Letter.

(*Page* 103, *lines* 23 and 24)

A transcript of the Letter.

THE SHADOW OF CAIN

(Page 105, line 9, to page 106, line 3)

'. . . the Point that flows
Till it becomes the line of Time . . . an endless positing
Of Nothing, or the Ideal that tries to burgeon
Into Reality through multiplying.'
— A reference to Oken, *op. cit.*

(Page 106, lines 5 and 6)

Arthur Rimbaud's *Metropolitan.*

(Page 108, line 13)

'. . . monstrous bull-voices of unseen fearful mimes.' — A fragment of
the lost play by Aeschylus, *The Edonians.*

(Page 108, line 17)

'Irenaeus expressed it so elegantly as it is almost pity if it be not true.
"*Inseminatus est ubique in Scripturis, Filius Dei,*" says he. The Son of God
is sowed in every furrow.' — John Donne, Sermon XI.

(Page 108, line 23)

Transcript of an actual report by an eye-witness of the bomb falling
on Hiroshima. — *The Times*, September 10, 1945.

(Page 109, lines 13, 14 and 16)

Founded on a passage in Burnet's *Theory of the Earth.*

(Page 110, lines 9 to 11)

These are references to descriptions given by Lombroso and Havelock
Ellis of the marks and appearance borne by prenatally disposed criminals.

(Page 110, lines 20 and 21)

'Also we must say that this or that is a disease of Gold, and not that it
is leprosy.' — *Paracelsus*, Appendix I, Chapter VI.

'Gold is the most noble of all, the most precious and primary metal.
. . . And we are not prepared to deny that leprosy, in all its forms, can be
thereby removed from the human frame.' — *Paracelsus.*

(*Page* 111, *lines* 4 to 9 and 10, 11)

These verses also contain references to Hermetic Writings.

(*Page* 111, *lines* 24 and 25)

John Donne, Sermon CXXXVI.

THE ROAD TO THEBES

(*Verses* 15 and 16)

bear reference to the Tibetan Book of the Dead.

(*Verse* 27, *lines* 1 and 2)

The Anatomy of Melancholy.

THE NIGHT WIND

(*Page* 123)

Final line inspired by a line from 'Altarwise by Owl-light,' by Dylan
Thomas:

'The world's my wound, God's Mary in her grief.'

THE DEATH OF PROMETHEUS

(*Page* 129, *lines* 11 and 12)

. . . No deserts hold
Beasts more desperate . . .
— Martinus Scriblerus

AT THE CROSSROADS

(Page 130, line 1)

was inspired by a phrase by Professor Martin Buber.

'HIS BLOOD COLOURS MY CHEEKS'

(Page 132, line 20)

'According to a statement of an ancient Chinese work of about 2000 B.C. a so-called man of the Hen Yeang Kingdom appears from his up-turned nose to be a snub-nosed monkey' (Rhinopithecus). — *Man as an Animal*, by W. C. Osman Hill, M.D., R.R.S.E. (Hutchinson University Library).

(Page 132, line 20)

'At one time, it was indeed the practice, in spite of their recognised and obvious connection with man, for apes and monkeys to be called *Quadramana*, or four-handed ones (and) to relegate man to a separate order called *Bimania* (i.e. two-handed).' — *op. cit.*

INDEX OF FIRST LINES